GRADES PreK-3

Dec. 2015

JULY/AUGUST
Monthly Idea Book

Ready-to-Use Templates, Activities, Management Tools, and More—for Every Day of the Month

Karen Sevaly

New York • Toronto • London • Auckland • Sydney
Mexico City • New Delhi • Hong Kong • Buenos Aires

Teaching *Resources*

DEDICATION
This book is dedicated to teachers and children everywhere.

Scholastic Inc. grants teachers permission to photocopy the reproducible pages from this book for classroom use.
No other part of this publication may be reproduced in whole or in part, or stored in a retrieval system, or transmitted
in any form or by any means, electronic, mechanical, photocopying, recording, or otherwise, without permission of the
publisher. For information regarding permission, write to Scholastic Inc., 557 Broadway, New York, NY 10012.

Cover design by Maria Lilja
Cover art by Jillian Phillips
Interior design by Holly Grundon
Illustrations by Karen Sevaly

ISBN 978-0-545-37943-4

1 2 3 4 5 6 7 8 9 10   40   19 18 17 16 15 14 13

CONTENTS

FAVORITE TOPICS

INDEPENDENCE DAY!

Reproducible Patterns

THE WILD WEST

Reproducible Patterns

OUR SOLAR SYSTEM

Reproducible Patterns

GOOD AND NUTRITIOUS!

AWARDS, INCENTIVES, AND MORE

ANSWER KEY

INTRODUCTION

Welcome to the original Monthly Idea Book series! This book was written especially for teachers getting ready to teach topics related to the months of July and August.

Each book in this month-by-month series is filled with dozens of ideas for PreK–3 classrooms. Activities connect to the Common Core State Standards for Reading (Foundational Skills), among other subjects, to help you meet the needs of your students. (For more information, see page 16.)

Most everything you need to prepare the lessons and activities in this resource is included, such as:

- calendar and weather-related props

- book cover patterns and stationery for writing assignments

- booklet patterns

- games and puzzles that support learning in curriculum areas such as math, science, and writing

- activity sheets that help students organize information, respond to learning, and explore topics in a meaningful way

- patterns for projects that connect to holidays, special occasions, and commemorative events

All year long, you can weave the ideas and reproducible patterns in these unique books into your monthly lesson plans and classroom activities. Happy teaching!

What's Inside

You'll find that this book is chockfull of reproducibles that make lesson planning easier:

■ puppets and picture props

■ book covers

■ game boards, puzzles, and word finds

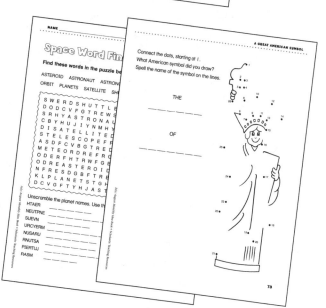

■ stationery

■ awards and certificates

How to Use This Book

The reproducible pages in this book have flexible use and may be modified to meet your particular classroom needs. Use the reproducible activity pages and patterns in conjunction with the suggested activities provided or weave them into your curriculum in other ways.

★ PHOTOCOPY OR SCAN

To get started, think about your developing lesson plans and upcoming bulletin boards. If desired, carefully remove the pages you will need. Duplicate those pages on copy paper, color paper, tagboard, or overhead transparency sheets. If you have access to a scanner, consider saving the pattern pages as PDF files. That way you can size images up or down and customize them with text to create individualized lessons, center-time activities, interactive whiteboard lessons, homework pages, and more.

★ LAMINATE FOR DURABILITY

Laminating the reproducibles will help you extend their use. If you have access to a roll laminator, then you already know how fortunate you are when it comes to saving time and resources. If you don't have a laminator, clear adhesive vinyl covering works well. Just sandwich the pattern between two sheets of vinyl and cut off any excess. Then try some of these ideas:

- Put laminated sheets of stationery in a writing center to use for handwriting practice. Wipe-off markers work great on coated pages and can easily be erased with dry tissue.

- Add longevity to calendars, weather-related pictures, and pocket chart rebus pictures by preserving them with lamination.

- Transform picture props into flannel board figures. After lamination, add a tab of hook-and-loop fastener to the back of the props and invite students to adhere them to the flannel board for storytelling fun.

- To enliven magnet board activities, affix sections of magnet tape to the back of picture props. Then encourage students to sort images according to the skills you're working on. For example, you might have them group images by commonalities such as initial sound, habitat, or physical attributes.

★ BULLETIN BOARDS

1. Set the Stage

Use background paper colors that complement many themes and seasons. For example, the dark background you use as a spooky display in October will have dramatic effect in November, when you begin a unit on woodland animals or Thanksgiving.

While paper works well, there are other background options available. You might also try fabric from a colorful bed sheet or gingham material. Discontinued rolls of patterned wallpaper can be purchased at discount stores. What's more, newspapers are easy to use and readily available. Attach a background of comics to set off a lesson on riddles, or use grocery store flyers to provide food for thought on a bulletin board about nutrition.

2. Make the Display

The reproducible patterns in this book can be enlarged to fit your needs. When we say enlarge, we mean it! Think BIG! Use an overhead projector to enlarge the images you need to make your bulletin board extraordinary.

If your school has a stencil press, you're lucky. The rest of us can use these strategies for making headers and titles.

- Cut strips of paper, cloud shapes, or cartoon bubbles. They will all look great! Then, by hand, write the text using wide-tipped permanent markers or tempera paint.

- If you must cut individual letters, use 4- by 6-inch pieces of construction paper. (Laminate first, if you can.) Cut the uppercase letters as shown on page 14. No need to measure, as somewhat irregular letters will look creative, not messy.

3. Add Color and Embellishments

Use your imagination! You'll be surprised at the great
displays you can create.

- Watercolor markers work great on
  small areas. On larger areas, you
  can switch to crayons, color chalk, or
  pastels. (Lamination will keep the color
  off of you. No laminator? A little hairspray
  will do the trick as a fixative.)

- Cut character eyes and teeth from white paper and glue them in
  place. The features will really stand out and make your bulletin
  boards engaging.

- For special effects, include items that provide texture and visual
  interest, such as buttons, yarn, and lace. Try cellophane or blue
  glitter glue on water scenes. Consider using metallic wrapping
  paper or aluminum foil to add a bit of shimmer to stars and
  belt buckles.

- Finally, take a picture of your completed bulletin board. Store the
  photos in a recipe box or large sturdy envelope. Next year when
  you want to create the same display, you'll know right where
  everything goes. You might even want to supply students with
  pushpins and invite them to recreate the display, following your
  directions and using the photograph as support.

Staying Organized

Organizing materials with monthly file folders provides you with a location to save reproducible activity pages and patterns, along with related craft ideas, recipes, and magazine or periodical articles.

If you prefer, use file boxes instead of folders. You'll find that with boxes there will plenty of room to store enlarged patterns, sample art projects, bulletin board materials, and much more.

Meeting the Standards

CONNECTIONS TO THE COMMON CORE STATE STANDARDS

The Common Core State Standards Initiative (CCSSI) has outlined learning expectations in English/Language Arts, among other subject areas, for students at different grade levels. In general, the activities in this book align with the following standards for students in grades K–3. For more information, visit the CCSSI website at www.corestandards.org.

Reading: Foundational Skills

Print Concepts
- RF.K.1, RF.1.1. Demonstrate understanding of the organization and basic features of print.

Phonics and Word Recognition
- RF.K.3, RF.1.3, RF.2.3, RF.3.3. Know and apply grade-level phonics and word analysis skills in decoding words.

Fluency
- RF.K.4. Read emergent-reader texts with purpose and understanding.
- RF.1.4, RF.2.4, RF.3.4. Read with sufficient accuracy and fluency to support comprehension.

Writing

Production and Distribution of Writing
- W.3.4. Produce writing in which the development and organization are appropriate to task and purpose.
- W.K.5, W.1.5, W.2.5, W.3.5. Focus on a topic and strengthen writing as needed by revising and editing.

Research to Build and Present Knowledge
- W.K.7, W.1.7, W.2.7. Participate in shared research and writing projects.
- W.3.7. Conduct short research projects that build knowledge about a topic.
- W.K.8, W.1.8, W.2.8, W.3.8. Recall information from experiences or gather information from provided sources to answer a question.

Range of Writing
- W.3.10. Write routinely over extended time frames (time for research, reflection, and revision) and shorter time frames (a single sitting or a day or two) for a range of discipline-specific tasks, purposes, and audiences.

Speaking & Listening

Comprehension and Collaboration
- SL.K.1, SL.1.1, SL.2.1. Participate in collaborative conversations with diverse partners about grade-level topics and texts with peers and adults in small and larger groups.
- SL.K.2, SL.1.2, SL.2.2, SL.3.2. Recount or describe key ideas or details from a text read aloud or information presented orally or through other media.
- SL.K.3, SL.1.3, SL.2.3, SL.3.3. Ask and answer questions about what a speaker says in order to gather additional information or clarify something that is not understood.

Presentation of Knowledge and Ideas
- SL.K.4, SL.1.4, SL.2.4. Describe people, places, things, and events with relevant details, expressing ideas and feelings clearly.
- SL.K.5, SL.1.5, SL.2.5, SL.3.5. Add drawings or other visual displays to stories or recounts of experiences when appropriate to clarify ideas, thoughts, and feelings.

Language

Conventions of Standard English
- L.K.1, L.1.1, L.2.1, L.3.1. Demonstrate command of the conventions of standard English grammar and usage when writing or speaking.
- L.K.2, L.1.2, L.2.2, L.3.2. Demonstrate command of the conventions of standard English capitalization, punctuation, and spelling when writing.

Knowledge of Language
- L.2.3, L.3.3. Use knowledge of language and its conventions when writing, speaking, reading, or listening.

Vocabulary Acquisition and Use
- L.K.4, L.1.4, L.2.4, L.3.4. Determine or clarify the meaning of unknown and multiple-meaning words and phrases based on grade level reading and content, choosing flexibly from an array of strategies.
- L.K.6, L.1.6, L.2.6, L.3.6. Use words and phrases acquired through conversations, reading and being read to, and responding to texts.

CALENDAR TIME

Getting Started

July

Sunday	Monday	Tuesday	Wednesday	Thursday	Friday	Saturday

August

Sunday	Monday	Tuesday	Wednesday	Thursday	Friday	Saturday

★ MARK YOUR CALENDAR

Make photocopies of the calendar grid on page 19 or 20 (depending on the current month) and use it to meet your needs. Consider using the write-on spaces to:

- write the corresponding numerals for each day

- mark and count how many days have passed

- track the weather with stamps or stickers

- note student birthdays

- record homework assignments

- communicate with families about positive behaviors

- remind volunteers about schedules, field trips, shortened days, and so on

★ CELEBRATIONS THIS MONTH

Whether you post a photocopy of pages 21–24 or pages 25–28 near your class calendar or just turn to these pages for inspiration, you're sure to find lots of information on them to discuss with students. To take celebrating and learning a step further, invite the class to add more to the list. For example, students can add anniversaries of significant events and the birthdays of their favorite authors or historical figures.

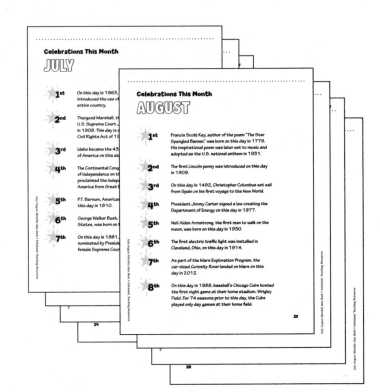

★ CALENDAR HEADER

You can make a photocopy of the header on page 29 or 30, color it, and use it as a title for your classroom calendar. You might opt to give the coloring job to a student who has a birthday that month. The student is sure to enjoy seeing his or her artwork each and every day of the month.

★ BEFORE INTRODUCING WHAT'S THE WEATHER?

Make a photocopy of the body template on page 31. Laminate it so you can use it again and again. Before sharing the template with the class, cut out pieces of cloth in the shapes of clothing students typically wear this month. For example, if you live in a warm weather climate, your summer attire might include shorts and t-shirts. If you live in chillier climates, your attire might include jeans, long sleeves, and a hat. Fit the cutouts to the body outline. When the clothing props are made, and you're ready to have students dress the template, display the clothing. Invite the "weather helper of the day" to tell what pieces of clothing he or she would choose to dress appropriately for the weather. (For extra fun, use foam to cut out accessories such as an umbrella, sunhat, and raincoat.)

July

Sunday	Monday	Tuesday	Wednesday	Thursday	Friday	Saturday

					Sunday	
					Monday	
					Tuesday	
					Wednesday	**August**
					Thursday	
					Friday	
					Saturday	

Celebrations This Month

JULY

1st On this day in 1963, the United States Post Office introduced the use of zip codes on mail for the entire country.

2nd Thurgood Marshall, the first African American U.S. Supreme Court Justice, was born on this day in 1908. This day is also the anniversary of the Civil Rights Act of 1964.

3rd Idaho became the 43rd state of the United States of America on this day in 1890.

4th The Continental Congress adopted the Declaration of Independence on this day in 1776. This document proclaimed the independence of the United States of America from Great Britain.

5th P.T. Barnum, American circus showman, was born on this day in 1810.

6th George Walker Bush, the 43rd President of the United States, was born on this day in 1946.

7th On this day in 1981, Sandra Day O'Connor was nominated by President Ronald Reagan to be the first female Supreme Court Justice in U.S. history.

8th The Liberty Bell rung out on this day in 1776 to summon citizens to the first public reading of the Declaration of Independence, which had been adopted just a few days earlier.

9th Today marks the birth date of American inventor Elias Howe, Jr., born in 1819. Howe patented the sewing machine, which helped revolutionize the garment industry.

10th American artist James McNeill Whistler, famously known for creating the painting *Whistler's Mother*, was born on this day in 1834.

11th *Charlotte's Web* author E.B. White was born on this day in 1899. White also wrote *Stuart Little*.

12th George Eastman, inventor of roll film for cameras and founder of the Eastman Kodak Company, was born on this day in 1854.

13th The Continental Congress enacted the Northwest Ordinance on this day in 1787, establishing rules for governing the Northwest Territory as well as procedures for admitting new states to the union.

14th On this day in 1969, these high-denomination currency notes were officially taken out of circulation: the $500, $1,000, $5,000, and $10,000 bills. Today, bills are printed in denominations of $1, $2, $5, $10, $20, $50, and $100.

15th The Ford Motor Company took its first order on this day in 1903. A week later, the company delivered the car to its customer, a dentist from Chicago, Illinois.

16th *Apollo 11*, the first U.S. lunar landing mission, was launched on this day in 1969. Astronauts Buzz Aldrin, Neil Armstrong, and Michael Collins manned the mission.

17th Disneyland, Walt Disney's first amusement park, was opened in Anaheim, California, on this day in 1955.

18th John Glenn, Jr., American astronaut and politician, was born on this day in 1921. Glenn was the first American to orbit the Earth.

19th The first women's rights convention was held in Seneca Falls, New York, on this day in 1848.

20th On this day in 1969, American astronaut Neil Armstrong became the first human to walk on the surface of the moon.

21st Janet Reno, the first female Attorney General of the United States, was born on this day in 1938.

22nd Born on this day in 1849, American poet Emma Lazarus became best known for authoring the sonnet engraved on the pedestal of the Statue of Liberty.

23rd On this day in 1962, *Telstar I*, the first communications satellite to be launched into space, relayed the first live transatlantic television broadcast and the first telephone call to be transmitted through space.

24th The discovery of Machu Picchu, an ancient Inca settlement in Peru, was announced on this day in 1911. This "City of the Incas" was voted one of the New Seven Wonders of the World in 2007.

25th Today is the birth date of Ruth Krauss, author of the beloved children's book *The Carrot Seed*. She was born in 1901.

26th On this day in 1788, New York became the eleventh province to ratify the United States Constitution and be admitted as an official state of the union.

27th U.S. figure skater and Olympic gold medalist Peggy Fleming was born on this day in 1948.

28th British children's author Beatrix Potter, writer of *The Tale of Peter Rabbit*, was born on this day in 1866.

29th The United States Congress established the National Aeronautics and Space Administration (NASA) on this day in 1958.

30th Today is the birth date of Henry Ford, American automobile manufacturer and founder of the Ford Motor Company. He was born in 1863.

31st British writer J.K. Rowling, author of the *Harry Potter* book series, was born on this day in 1965.

Celebrations This Month

AUGUST

1st Francis Scott Key, author of the poem "The Star Spangled Banner," was born on this day in 1779. His inspirational poem was later set to music and adopted as the U.S. national anthem in 1931.

2nd The first Lincoln penny was introduced on this day in 1909.

3rd On this day in 1492, Christopher Columbus set sail from Spain on his first voyage to the New World.

4th President Jimmy Carter signed a law creating the Department of Energy on this day in 1977.

5th Neil Alden Armstrong, the first man to walk on the moon, was born on this day in 1930.

6th The first electric traffic light was installed in Cleveland, Ohio, on this day in 1914.

7th As part of the Mars Exploration Program, the car-sized *Curiosity Rover* landed on Mars on this day in 2012.

8th On this day in 1988, baseball's Chicago Cubs hosted the first night game at their home stadium, Wrigley Field. For 74 seasons prior to this day, the Cubs played only day games at their home field.

9th As part of its fire prevention campaign, the United States Forest Service released the first poster featuring Smokey Bear on this day in 1944.

10th The Smithsonian Institution, a group of museums and research centers, was established on this day in 1846 "for the increase and diffusion of knowledge."

11th Baseball legend Babe Ruth became the first player to hit 500 home runs on this day in 1929.

12th American songwriter Katherine Lee Bates, who wrote the words to "America the Beautiful," was born on this day in 1859.

13th On this day in 2008, swimmer Michael Phelps won his eighth gold medal, setting the record for gold medals won by an individual at any single Olympics Games.

14th Today marks the anniversary of the end of World War II, which was announced in 1945.

15th The Hollywood premiere of *The Wizard of Oz* was held at Grauman's Chinese Theatre on this day in 1939.

16th On this day in 1896, gold was discovered near the Klondike River in the Yukon Territory of Canada. Before long, "Klondike Fever" lured tens of thousands of gold seekers to the region in the hopes of striking it rich.

17th American frontiersman and politician Davy Crockett, also known as "King of the Wild Frontier," was born on this day in 1786.

18th In Roanoke Colony on this day in 1587, Virginia Dare became the first English child born in colonial America.

19th Aviation pioneer Orville Wright was born on this day in 1871. He and his older brother, Wilbur, invented and flew the first successful airplane in Kill Devil Hills, North Carolina.

20th Italian mountain climber Reinhold Messner made the first successful solo climb of Mount Everest on this day in 1980.

21st Hawaii became the 50th state of the United States of America on this day in 1959.

22nd The International Red Cross was established in Geneva, Switzerland on this day in 1864.

23rd Today is the birth date of American dancer, choreographer, and actor Gene Kelly, born in 1912.

24th Mount Vesuvius erupted on this day in 79 A.D., burying the Roman cities of Pompeii and Herculaneum under thick layers of volcanic matter. These ancient civilizations were rediscovered and the remains excavated in the 18th century.

25th Leonard Bernstein, American composer and conductor, was born on this day in 1918.

26th The 19th Amendment, giving women the right to vote, was adopted into the U.S. Constitution on this day in 1920.

27th Lyndon Baines Johnson, 36th president of the United States, was born on this day in 1908.

28th Today marks the anniversary of the March on Washington, held in 1963. This civil rights event culminated in the famous "I Have a Dream" speech given by Martin Luther King, Jr., on the steps of the Lincoln Memorial.

29th American recording artist and entertainer Michael Jackson, also known as the King of Pop, was born on this day in 1958.

30th On this day in 1983, Guion S. Bluford became the first African American to travel into space. He was one of five crewmembers on the *Challenger* and participated in the first night launch of a space shuttle.

31st Italian physician and educator Maria Montessori, developer of the Montessori method of education, was born on this day in 1870.

SUMMER FUN, SUMMER TREATS

In July and August, the days of summer are in full bloom. As children enjoy the wonders of the warm outdoors and relaxing vacation days, they're sure to also appreciate some popular summer treats to fill their tummies and keep them cool. Use the summer-related activities in this unit to reinforce learning and help keep students' skills sharp for the upcoming school year.

Suggested Activities

★ A FIELD OF SUNFLOWERS

Invite students to make a field of sunflowers to celebrate these popular summer blooms. To begin, provide small, yellow paper plates, yellow construction paper, sunflower seeds, and white glue. Ask students to cut out a supply of triangle-shaped petals from the construction paper. Have them glue their petals around the rim of a paper plate. For the seedy center of their flower, have students glue a handful of sunflower seeds onto the plate. After the glue dries, students can cut out green construction-paper leaves and long stems and then assemble the pieces with their flower to create a tall sunflower plant. Finally, help students attach their sunflowers to a bulletin board to create a fantastic summer display. (If desired, they might make insects from craft items to add to the display.)

★ SUN PAPER-BAG PUPPET

Students can make this sunny puppet to use in role-playing, to share information about their summer activities, or just for fun! Distribute small paper bags and photocopies of the patterns on page 37. Ask students to color and cut out the sun patterns. Then have them glue the eye section of the sun to the bottom flap of the bag and the mouth section to the front of the bag below the flap.

★ SUNSHINE MESSAGES

Use this idea to share positive messages and praise with students, or to track students' accomplishments or behavior. Photocopy a sun (page 38) and at least eight sunrays (page 39) for each student. You might use yellow paper. Have students cut out their sun and label it with their name. Then display the suns on a bulletin board. Cut out the sunrays and place them in a basket near the display. Whenever you want to praise or encourage a student, simply write a message on a sunray and give it to the student. Or give the student a sunray whenever he or she completes an assignment or displays a desirable behavior. Have students glue each sunray to their sun. Once a student has collected and glued eight sunrays onto his or her sun, reward the student with a special treat or privilege.

★ GIANT SUMMER GLASSES

Have students make giant glasses to display on a bulletin board titled "See What a Great Summer We're Having!" To make templates, photocopy page 40 onto several sheets of tagboard and cut out the patterns. Then ask students to fold a sheet of light-colored construction paper in half and do the following:

1. Place a template along the fold where indicated. Trace around the shape. Then trace along the inner opening of the shape (this will be the lens of the glasses).

2. Cut out the shape through both layers of paper. Do not cut out the lens.

3. Unfold the cutout. Flip the template and trace the lens onto the other side to create a pair of large glasses.

4. Write about a summer activity or adventure on one lens. Draw a picture to go with the text on the other lens.

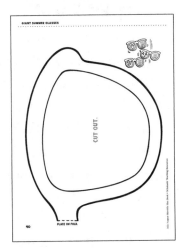

BAREFOOTIN'

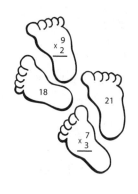

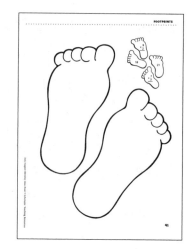

Summer is the ideal time for children to kick off their shoes and walk barefoot through a cool grassy field or along a soft, sandy beach. Photocopy a supply of the footprints on page 41, cut them out, and label them to reinforce a variety of skills. For example, label the footprint pairs with math facts, contractions, synonyms, word family words, and so on. Then place the footprints in a learning center for students to use as a matching activity or in a game of Memory.

SUMMER WRITING

Invite students to record their memorable summer time experiences with a variety of creative writing and publishing activities.

My Summer Journal

Photocopy a supply of page 42 and place in your writing center. Encourage students to use the sheets to write about things they did, saw, or learned about during the summer. If desired, students can cut apart the sections, glue each one to a sheet of paper, and add a drawing to go with the text. They can then bind their pages between construction-paper covers to make a full-size journal.

Summer Vacation

Distribute photocopies of page 43 for students to use when writing about their summer vacation or other summer activities. Or, they might write about their summer time musings, observations, or wishes. To encourage other kinds of creative writing, challenge students to write summer-related poetry, songs, acrostics, and so on. If desired, provide photocopies of the book cover (page 44) and have students create book covers for their written work. Students simply color and cut out the pattern and glue it to a folded sheet of 11- by 17-inch construction paper where indicated.

★ SUMMER TREAT ACTIVITIES

Photocopy and cut out a supply of the cone and scoop patterns (page 45), watermelon slices (page 46), and pizza and topping patterns (page 46) to use for activities such as the ones described below.

Ice Cream Cone

- Write math facts on the scoops and answers on the cones. Have students solve each math fact and match it to the corresponding cone.

- Label a three-column chart with ice cream flavors. Have students write their name on a scoop and place it on the chart under their favorite flavor. Tally and review the results with students. If desired, use the results to create a graph.

- Write contractions on the cones and the corresponding word pairs on the scoops. Have students match the scoops and cones.

Watermelon Slices

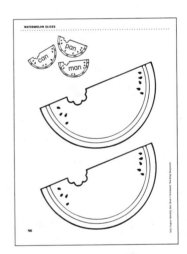

- Write content-related vocabulary on the cutouts and display on a word wall.

- Write a variety of word-family words on the slices (one word per slice). Have students group the words by word-family endings.

- Label each watermelon with a number. Then have students count out and place the corresponding number of watermelon seeds onto each slice.

Pizza and Toppings

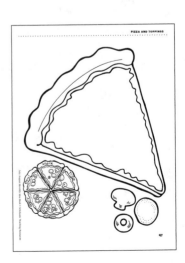

- Put together six cutouts to create a whole pizza. Use the slices to reinforce fraction concepts, such as whole, half, thirds, and sixths.

- Distribute the pizza cutouts to a small group. Have students add toppings according to your directions, such as "Put three pepperonis and two mushrooms on your slice."

- Write story starters on the cutouts and have students use them as prompts for their creative writing activities.

★ MY PIZZA RECIPE

Invite students to write the recipe for their favorite pizza on a photocopy of page 48. Or, they might write a recipe for a make-believe pizza, such as a pizza made of all red ingredients, or one made of nature items (rocks, leaves, flowers). Display students' completed recipes on a bulletin board titled "Our Pizza Creations."

★ SUMMER TREATS WRITING ACTIVITIES

Promote creative writing with the stationery on page 49. Invite students to write about their favorite treat: ice cream, watermelon, or pizza. They can describe that food, how they like to eat it, special ingredients that make the treat tastier, or fun ways to serve it. Or they might write an imaginary adventure involving their treat, even giving it human characteristics to add interest. Alternately, students might write poems, rhymes, or songs about their favorite treat. When finished, invite students to use the pattern of their choice (pages 50, 51, or 52) to make a cover for their written work. To make, students color and cut out the pattern and glue it to a folded sheet of 11- by 17-inch construction paper where indicated. They can customize their cover by writing a title and adding an author line.

★ SUMMER TREATS TASK CARDS

Reinforce the skills your students are learning with flash cards that fit the summer treat theme of this unit. Simply photocopy the cards on page 53 and cut them out. You can program the cutouts for use as flash cards to teach letters, numbers, math facts, content-area vocabulary words, sight words, and so on. The cards are ideal for learning-center activities, but you might also use them as labels for job charts, to group students, for nametags, and more. To store, just put them in a resealable plastic bag.

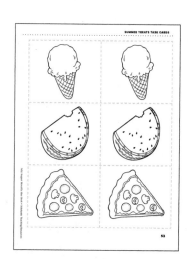

You Are My Sunshine!
Jeremy

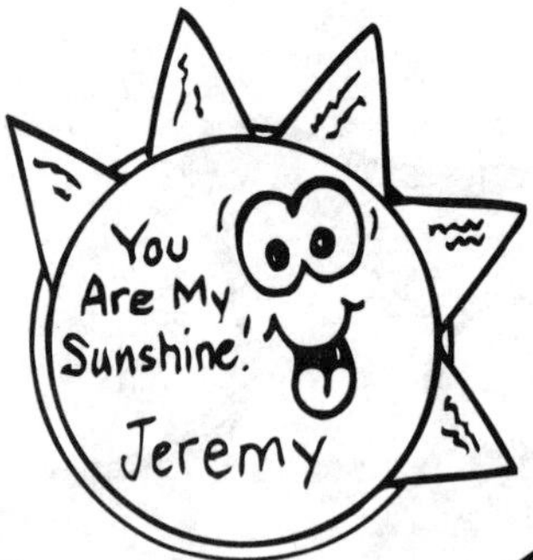

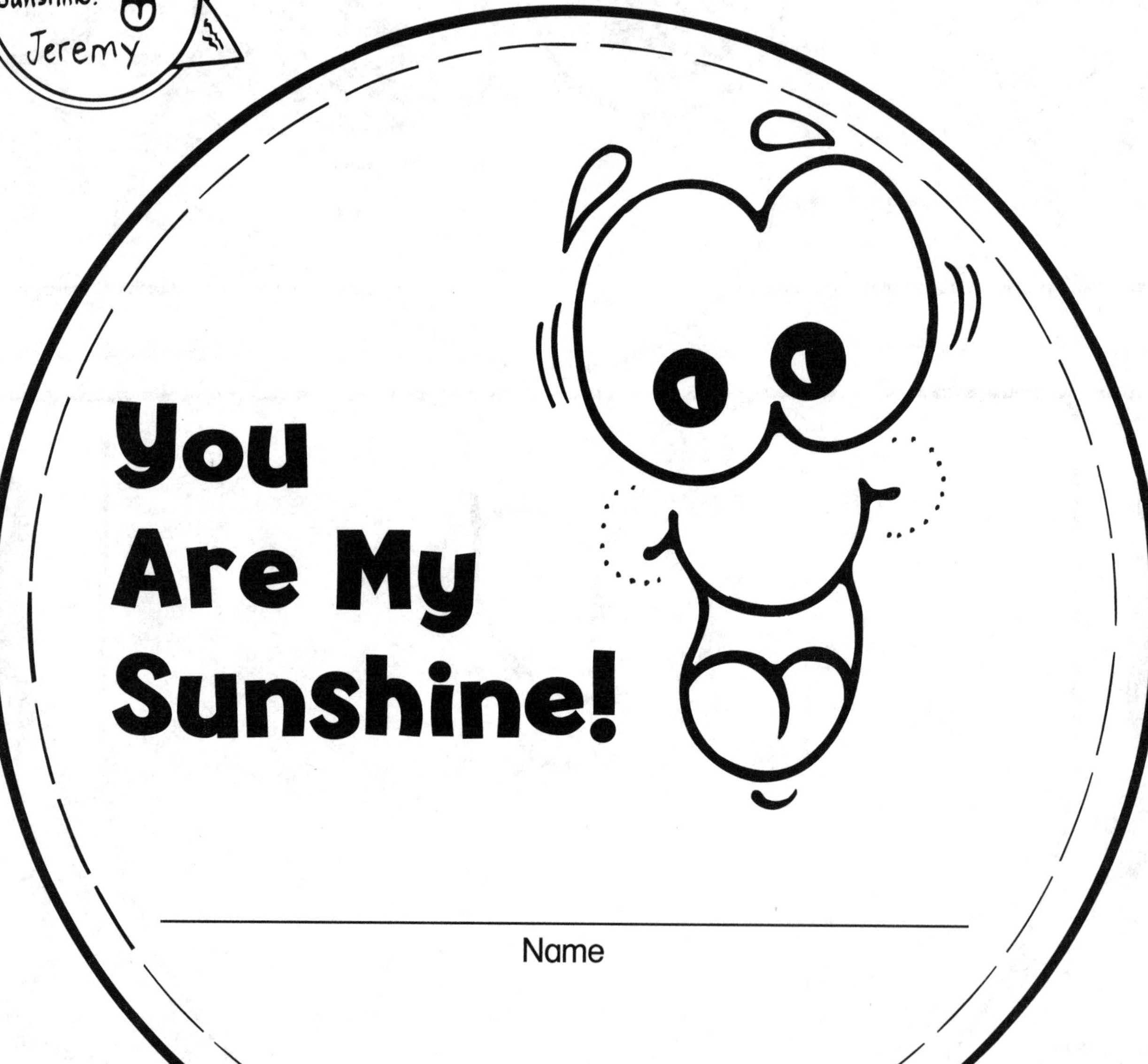

You Are My Sunshine!
Name

CUT OUT.

PLACE ON FOLD.

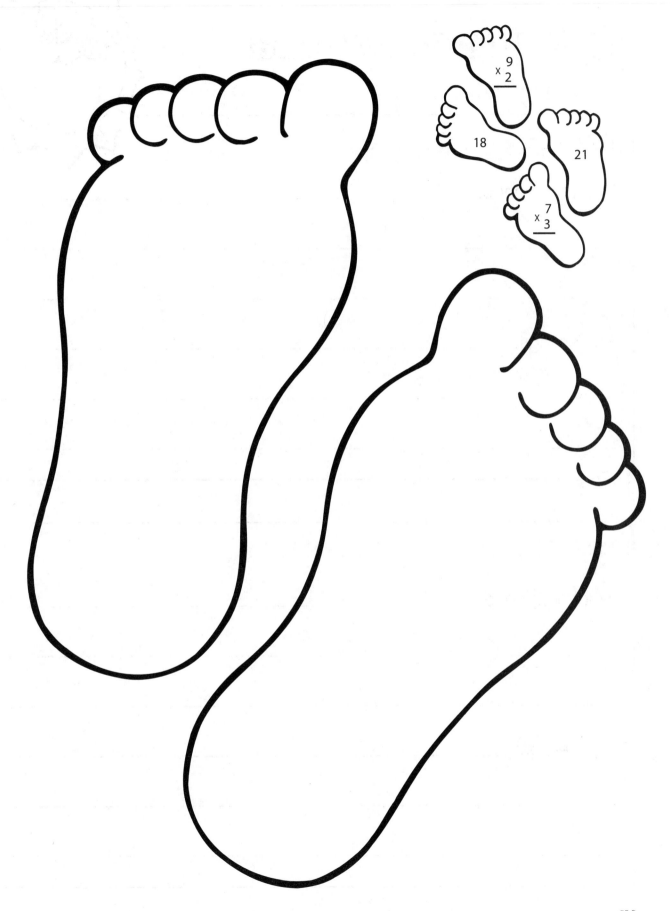

My Summer Journal

Date: _____

What happened: _____

_____

_____

_____

My feelings: _____

_____

_____

_____

Date: _____

What happened: _____

_____

_____

_____

My feelings: _____

_____

_____

July/August Monthly Idea Book © Scholastic Teaching Resources

My Summer Vacation

_____

- - - - - - - - - - - - - - - - -

_____

- - - - - - - - - - - - - - - - -

_____

- - - - - - - - - - - - - - - - -

_____

- - - - - - - - - - - - - - - - -

_____

- - - - - - - - - - - - - - - - -

_____

- - - - - - - - - - - - - -

_____

- - - - - - - - - - - - - -

_____

My Summer Book

Name

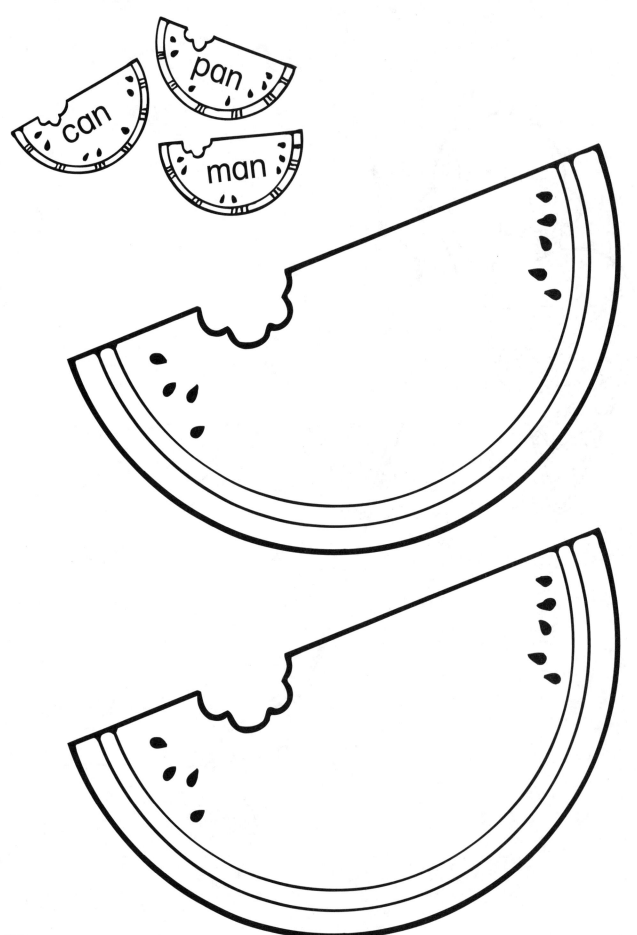

can

pan

man

My Pizza Recipe

My favorite type of pizza is: _____

Here's how to make it!

Step 1: _____

_____

Step 2: _____

_____

Step 3: _____

_____

Step 4: _____

_____

Bake the pizza at _____ degrees for _____ minutes.

Comments: _____

_____

_____

PLACE THIS SIDE ALONG FOLD.

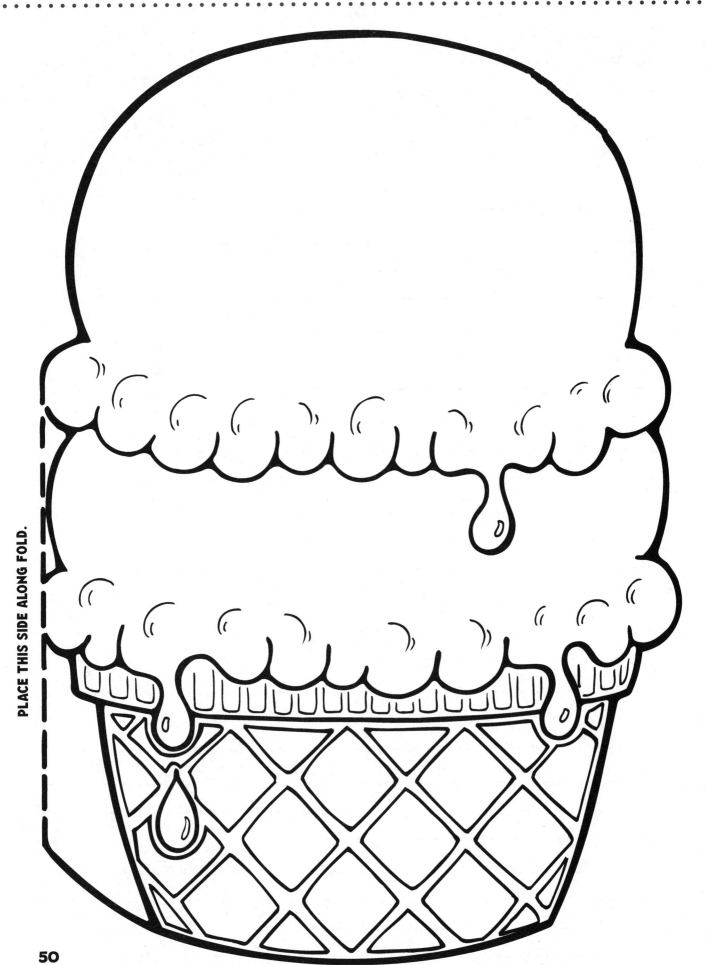

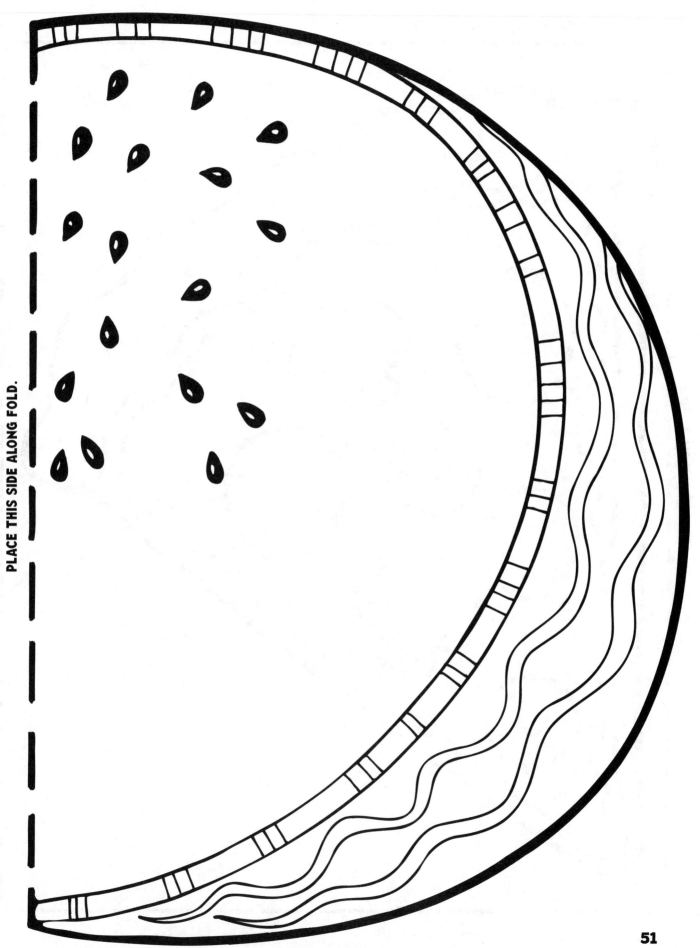

PLACE THIS SIDE ALONG FOLD.

PLACE THIS SIDE ALONG FOLD.

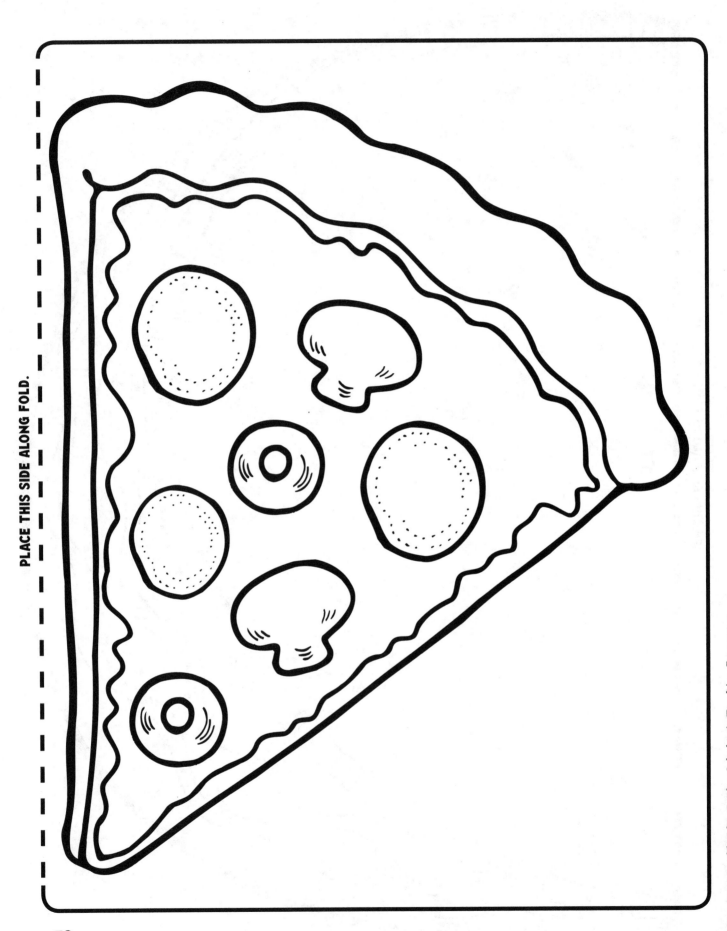

INDEPENDENCE DAY!

The anniversary of Independence Day, or the Fourth of July, is a significant time for citizens of the United States. This day marks the anniversary of the adoption of the Declaration of Independence by the Continental Congress in 1776. With this act, the thirteen original colonies formed a new nation, the United States of America.

Today, the Fourth of July is observed as a national holiday celebrated in many ways, including parades, picnics, and fireworks. While most celebrations are often fun and festive, this holiday also offers Americans an opportunity to remember the commitment and sacrifice of our forefathers to ensure the freedoms that we enjoy each day, making the United States the great nation that it is.

Declaration of Independence

The Declaration of Independence is a document that declared the rights of a new nation. It explained the feelings of the colonists and listed the wrongs they suffered under British rule. It also stated that the people of the United States would fight their own wars, make their own peace, and carry on their own trade. With the signing of this document, the United States became an independent, free nation.

Thomas Jefferson, with the help of Benjamin Franklin and John Adams, wrote the document. The first person to sign the Declaration of Independence was John Hancock, President of the Continental Congress. Fifty-six men in all signed the document. In signing, the men pledged "our lives, our fortunes, and our sacred honor" to each other and to their new country. One of the best-known sentences in the document is the second one which reads:

We hold these truths to be self-evident, that all men are created equal, that they are endowed by their Creator with certain unalienable Rights, that among these are Life, Liberty and the pursuit of Happiness.

Suggested Activities

★ PATRIOTIC FUN WORD FIND

Use the word find on page 61 to help students become familiar with Independence-Day-related vocabulary. After students complete the activity, have them use words from the puzzle in a creative writing exercise.

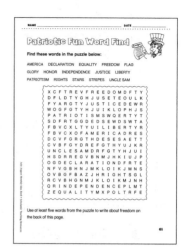

★ FREEDOM FIGHTERS

Invite students to research and write about one of our founding fathers, or another historical figure that had a significant role in helping Americans achieve freedom from British rule in colonial times. You might work with students to make a list of the signers of the Declaration of Independence from which students can choose their subject. Then distribute photocopies of page 62 to students. Have them choose a person to research and then use library books, the Internet, and other sources to gather information about their subject and to complete their report. Afterward, invite each student to share his or her report with the class. If desired, collect the reports and bind them together to make a student-created book to add your class library.

★ EAGLE PAPER-BAG PUPPET

Distribute small paper bags and photocopies of the patterns on page 63 to students. Then have them color and cut out the patterns. Instruct students to glue their eagle's head to the bottom flap of the bag and its mouth and body to the front of the bag below the flap. Students can use their completed puppets to present their "Freedom Fighters" report (see above) or to share what they have learned about the Declaration of Independence and the struggles of early Americans to secure their freedom from British rule.

PATRIOTIC SYMBOLS OF OUR COUNTRY

Patriotic symbols that represent our country play a prominent role in most July Fourth celebrations. American flags, Uncle Sam costumes and posters, and replicas of the Statue of Liberty are often seen along parade routes and at picnics and concerts. Red, white, and blue decorations abound, often featuring stars and stripes as seen on our flag. These colors are also commonly used in the fireworks displays that many cities hold to commemorate the anniversary of our country's independence. Students can make their own patriotic symbols to use in their presentations about Independence Day or to enjoy in their own July Fourth celebrations.

American Flag

Display an American flag, then discuss its colors and design with students. Explain that the thirteen red and white stripes represent the thirteen original colonies of the United States and that stars on the blue field represent the fifty states in our country. Invite students to share their thoughts about why the flag is a patriotic symbol. Then distribute photocopies of page 64 and invite students to color the flag, using the actual flag as a reference. When finished, have them write about what the flag means to them on the back.

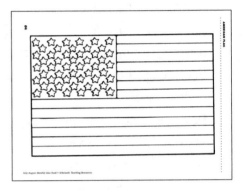

Uncle Sam Hat and Beard

To make an Uncle Sam hat, help students fit a 2 ½-inch wide construction-paper strip around their head and staple the ends together to create a headband. Then distribute photocopies of the hat pattern on page 65. Ask students to color their hat red, white, and blue. Finally, have them cut out the hat and staple (or glue) it to their headband.

For the Uncle Sam beard, have students cut out construction-paper copies of the beard pattern (page 66). To wear, they simply loop the ends of the beard around their ears.

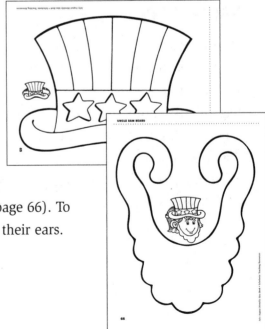

Statue of Liberty Torch

Invite students to make their own torch of freedom. To prepare, photocopy a class supply of the flame (page 67) onto red construction paper and the base (page 68) onto yellow construction paper. Give each student a set of patterns and a cardboard tube (paper towel tubes work well). Have students cut out their patterns and do the following to make their torch:

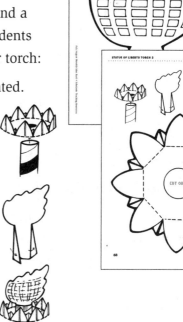

1. Cut out the center of the torch base where indicated. Then snip along each of the eight short, solid lines.

2. Fold up the rim of the base, as shown. Then slide the base over one end of the tube. Use tape to secure the base in place (about one inch from the end of the tube).

3. Fold the bottom of the flame along the lines. Fold one side forward and the other side back.

4. Fit the folded part of the flame into the top of the tube, as shown.

Crown

Students can wear this crown and use the torch (above) as part of their role-playing activities or just to strike a Lady Liberty pose to express their patriotism. Distribute 9-inch paper plates and construction-paper photocopies of page 69 to students. Have students cut out their crown spikes, then instruct them to do the following to make their crown:

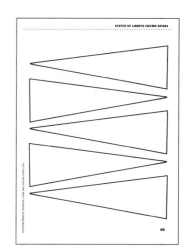

1. To make the crown band, cut off a section of the paper plate rim, then cut out the center of the plate, as shown. If desired, color the band.

2. Tape (or glue) the spikes to the crown band, as shown. Fold back each side of the band that extends beyond the spikes and tape in place.

3. To wear, fit the crown onto your head so that the spikes stand upright.

Stand-Up Uncle Sam and Lady Liberty

Distribute photocopies of the Uncle Sam and Lady Liberty stand-up character patterns on pages 70 and 71. Ask students to color and cut out each pattern. Then have them glue the flag to Uncle Sam's outstretched hand and the torch to Lady Liberty's raised hand. Finally, fold back each side of the cutouts and stand on a flat surface in front of a bulletin board covered in red, white, or blue paper (or a combination of these colors). To enhance the display, ask students to write facts about each of these patriotic symbols on large, plain index cards and attach them to the bulletin board.

Patriotic Finger Puppets

To make these quick-and-easy finger puppets, photocopy one pattern of each patriotic character puppet (page 72) for each student. Then have students color and cut out each puppet. Help them, as needed, to cut out the small circles on their puppets. To use, students simply slip their fingers into the holes and wiggle them around to serve as legs for their puppets.

★ A GREAT AMERICAN SYMBOL

Photocopy the connect-the-dot activity (page 73) and distribute to students. Explain that when they connect the dots, a famous American symbol will appear. After they reveal the symbol, have students fill in the letters to write its name. Afterward, they can color their picture and write what they know about the symbol on the back of their page.

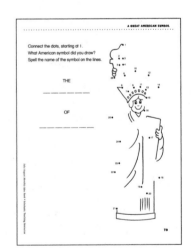

INDEPENDENCE DAY CREATIVE WRITING

Liven up students' writing with stationery ideal for writing about their July Fourth celebrations, the Declaration of Independence, patriotic symbols, or any other related topic. Students might write poems, songs, acrostics, or imaginary stories. Photocopy the stationery on pages 74, 75, and 76 for students to use for their final drafts. Then invite volunteers to share their written work with small groups or the whole class.

STATUE OF LIBERTY BOOK COVER

Invite students to use photocopies of page 77 to create book covers for their Independence Day writing assignments. To make, instruct students to color and cut out the book cover. Ask them to add a title and author line. Then have students fold a red, white, or blue sheet of 11- by 17-inch construction paper in half and glue their cover cutout to it, placing the left edge along the fold. Finally, help students staple their pages inside their cover.

UNCLE SAM PAGE FRAMER

Students can use this patriotic page framer to display writing assignments or artwork related to Independence Day. To begin, distribute photocopies of the patterns on pages 78–79. Ask students to color and cut out the patterns and glue them to the edges of a sheet of construction paper, as shown. Then have them attach their written work or drawing to the front of the page framer.

PATRIOTIC MOBILE

Invite students to construct these easy-to-make mobiles to display or use as a prop when sharing their Independence Day knowledge. First, give each student a photocopy of the mobile patterns (pages 80–82), two 1-foot lengths of yarn, and scissors. Also provide glue, a hole punch, and crayons. Then have students do the following to make their mobile:

1. Color and cut out the patterns.

2. On the back of each cutout, write a fact or something interesting about Independence Day.

3. Punch four holes in the star-topped banner and one hole near the top of each of the other cutouts where indicated.

4. Cut one of the 1-foot lengths of yarn into three strands of varying lengths, then tie one strand each to the hole in the eagle, scroll, and bell. Tie the other end of the strands to a hole at the bottom of the banner, as shown.

5. To make a hanger, tie the other 1-foot length of yarn to the hole in the top of the banner.

JULY FUN GLASSES

Invite students to make and wear a pair of glasses to celebrate the Fourth of July. Distribute copies of the glasses patterns on page 83. Ask students to color the patterns in patriotic colors. Then have them cut out the pieces, carefully cutting out the centers of the glasses and the slits on the glasses frame and the earpieces. To assemble, students simply fit each earpiece into the corresponding slit on the frame. If desired, students can take their glasses home to wear during their Independence Day festivities.

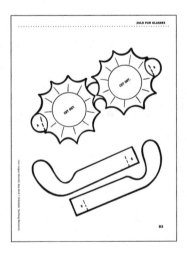

Patriotic Fun Word Find

Find these words in the puzzle below:

AMERICA   DECLARATION   EQUALITY   FREEDOM   FLAG

GLORY   HONOR   INDEPENDENCE   JUSTICE   LIBERTY

PATRIOTISM   RIGHTS   STARS   STRIPES   UNCLE SAM

```
X C F T R E V F R E E D O M D F T Y
D F L D T Y G H J U S E T E O U L K
F Y A R G T Y J U S T I C E D E W R
W O G F G T Y H J U I K L O P H J S
P A T R I O T I S M S W Q E R T Y T
S D F R T G G D E D S E W D S W T A
F B V C X L T Y U I L I B E R T Y R
F B V C X O F A M E R I C A D R E S
D C V F G R G T H D E S E S A E T T
C V B F G Y D R E F G T H Y U J K R
U N C L E S A M D R F G T Y H J U I
H S D R R E G V B N M J H K I U J P
O G D E C L A R A T I O N D F R T E
N F V G B H N J M K L O I K J M N S
O V B G F B A Z J H R I G H T S G L
R C V B H G N M J K L O I K M J N H
Q R I N D E P E N D E N C E P L M T
Z E Q U A L I T Y M X P O L T R F E
```

Use at least five words from the puzzle to write about freedom on the back of this page.

My Freedom-Fighter Report

My freedom fighter is _____

_____

Birth date: _____

Birth place: _____

_____

This person helped promote freedom by _____

_____

_____

Some ways this freedom fighter helped others are: ____

_____

_____

The most important contribution this person made is ____

_____

_____

If I could meet my freedom fighter, I would: _____

_____

_____

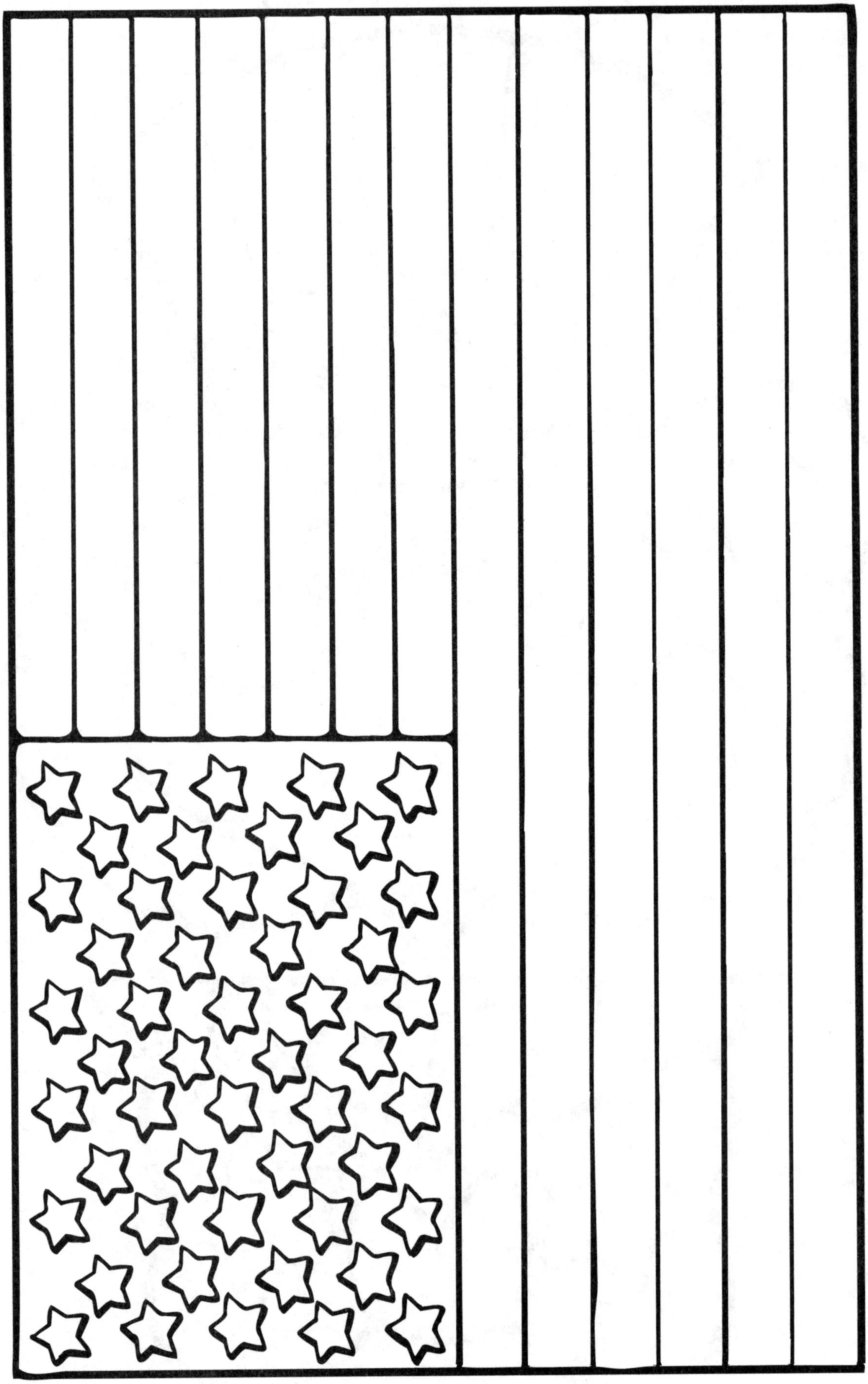

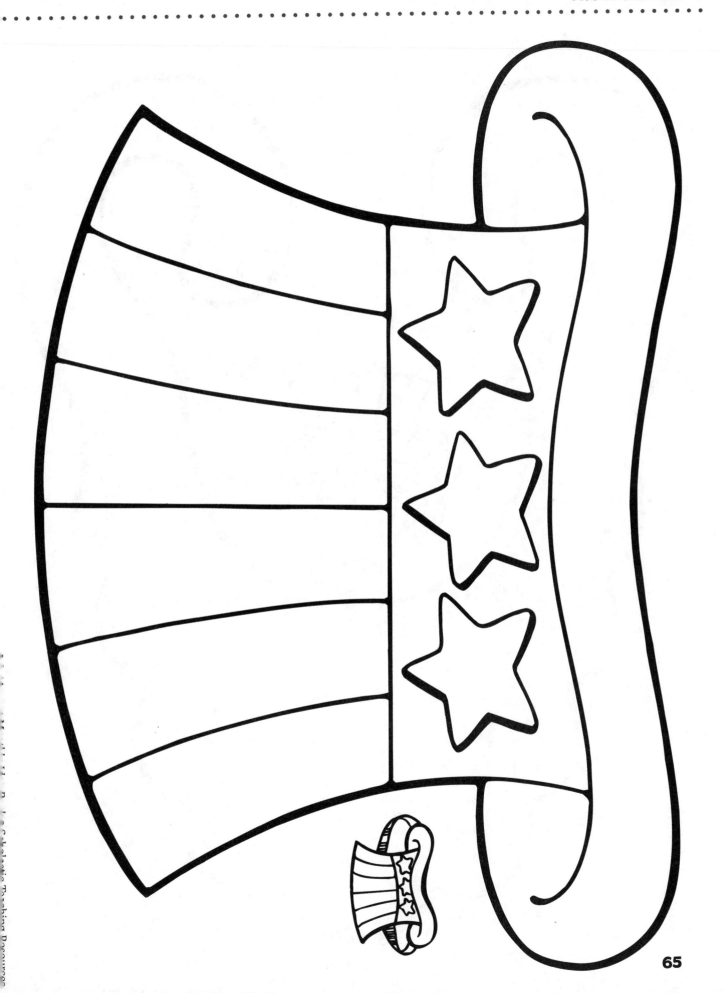

CUT OUT.

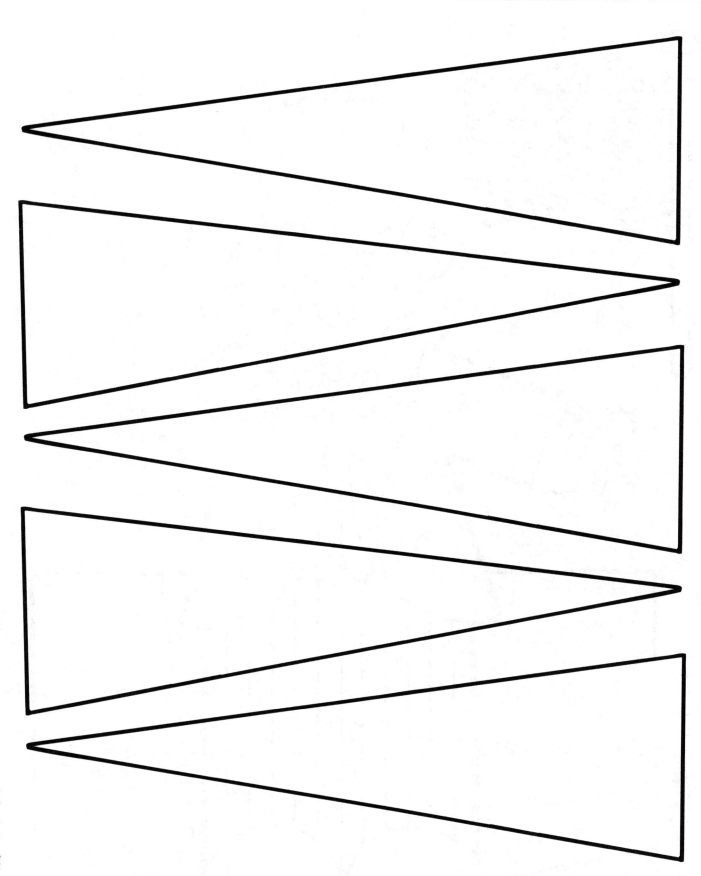

July/August Monthly Idea Book © Scholastic Teaching Resources

July/August Monthly Idea Book © Scholastic Teaching Resources

Connect the dots, starting at 1.

What American symbol did you draw?

Spell the name of the symbol on the lines.

THE

___ ___ ___ ___ ___ ___

OF

___ ___ ___ ___ ___ ___ ___

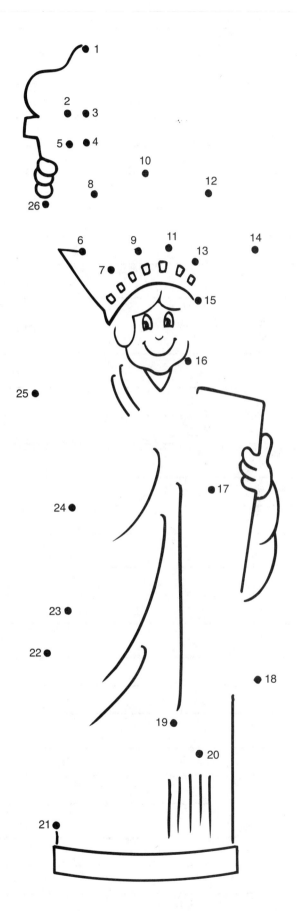

_____

- - - - - - - - - - - - - - - - - - - -

_____

- - - - - - - - - - - - - - - - - - - -

_____

- - - - - - - - - - - - - - - - - - - -

_____

- - - - - - - - - - - - - - - - - - - -

_____

- - - - - - - - - - - - - - - - - - - -

_____

- - - - - - - - - - - - - - - - - - - -

_____

- -

_____

- -

_____

- -

_____

- -

_____

July/August Monthly Idea Book © Scholastic Teaching Resources

PLACE THIS SIDE ALONG FOLD.

July/August Monthly Idea Book © Scholastic Teaching Resources

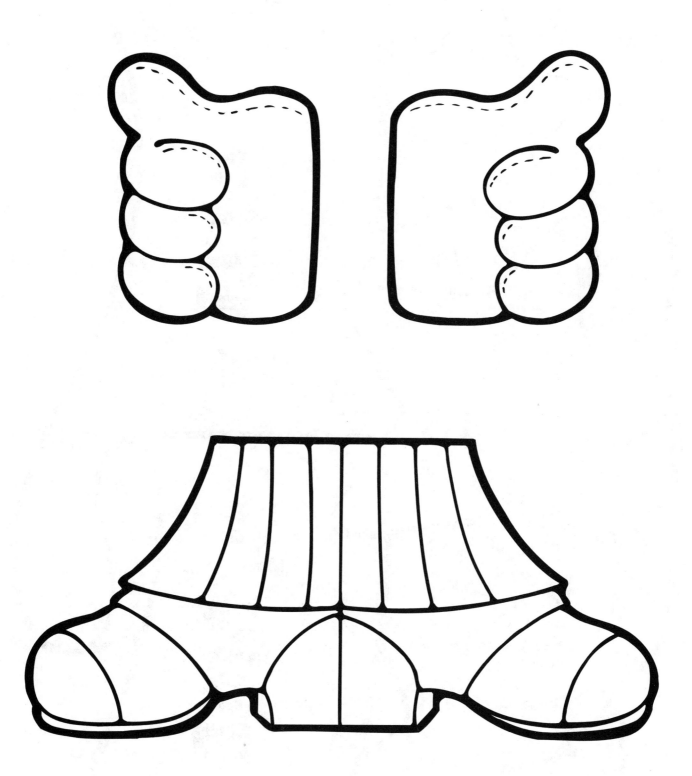

1776

July 4,

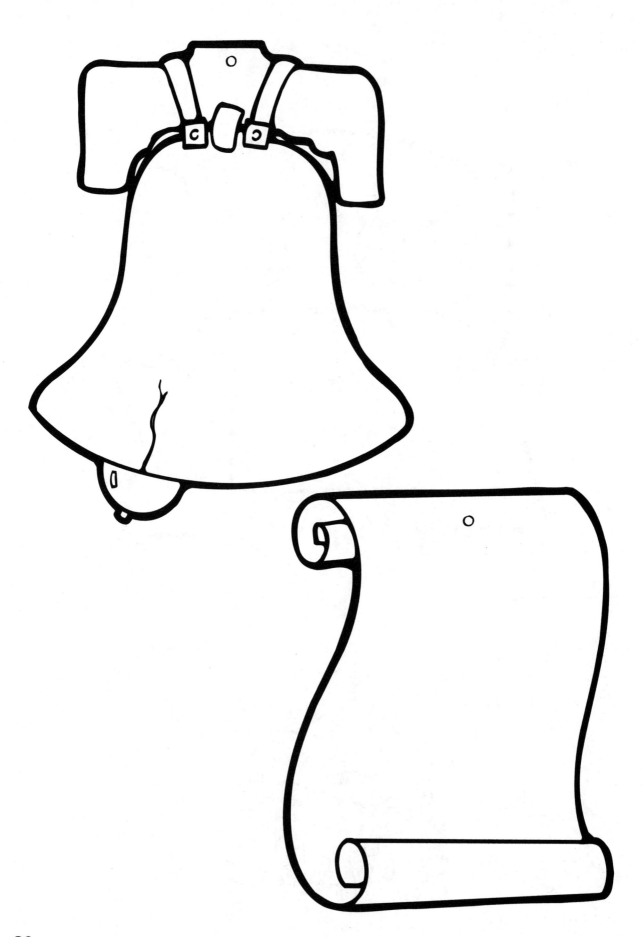

THE WILD WEST

As American settlers expanded westward during the 1800s, the need for cowhands—or cowboys—developed and grew. In the frontier days, cowboys herded, branded, and drove cattle, and did a number of other ranch-related jobs. The work required physical ability, specific skills, and special clothes and equipment. Typically, men worked as cowhands, but some women also took on the tasks and learned the necessary skills to earn the title of "cowgirl." Modern cowboys do many of the same types of jobs as their Wild West predecessors, but advances in equipment and techniques have made some of their responsibilities easier to perform. In this unit, the term "cowboy" is used to refer to both male and female cowhands.

Suggested Activities

★ COWBOY LIFE

Invite students to share what they know about cowboys. You might make a list of cowboy-related words to review and include in the discussion. Afterward, have students do research to learn more about the history, traditions, and lifestyles of cowboys. They can use classroom, library, and Internet resources as well as videos, personal interviews, and other helpful sources to gather their information. If desired, have students work in pairs or small groups and assign a different topic to each group to research, such as the equipment cowboys use, what they wear, and types of jobs they do. You might also have students compare cowboys from the frontier days to modern-day cowboys. Distribute photocopies of the stationery on page 88 for students to use when writing the final draft of their findings. They can then use photocopies of page 89 to prepare a cover for their written work. Have students color and cut out the pattern, glue it to a folded sheet of 11- by 17-inch construction paper where indicated, then add a title and name line.

★ HORSE PAGE FRAMER

Encourage students to write short stories, skits, poems, songs, or other texts about the Wild West, cowboys, life on the trail, or related topics. When finished, distribute photocopies of page 90 and ask students to color and cut out the horse patterns. To make a page framer, have them glue the horse's head to the top edge of a sheet of construction paper, the tail to the bottom edge, and the hooves to the side edges. Finally, have students attach their written work to the front of the page framer.

★ WILD WEST PROPS

Students will enjoy making the following props to use in their Wild-West presentations or dramatizations.

Hinged Horse

For this moveable horse, photocopy pages 91–92 for each student. Then distribute the pages and have students color and cut out the horse patterns. Next, have them use four brass fasteners to attach their horse's head, tail, and legs to the body where indicated. If desired, invite students to glue a wide craft stick to the back of the horse to use as a puppet handle. Then they can move their horse in a variety of ways to make it dance or to spin and wiggle its limbs in amusing ways.

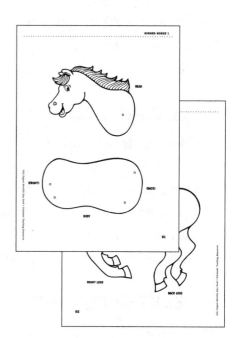

Ten-Gallon Hat

Distribute photocopies of the hat pattern (page 93) to students to color and cut out. Next, have them staple their cutout to a 2- by 24-inch strip of brown construction paper. To complete, help students fit the strip to their head, stapling the ends together and trimming the excess.

Spurs

To make spurs, give each student two photocopies of page 94. Ask them to color and cut out their patterns. To assemble, have students glue each pair of cutouts together at the tab, matching the ends marked with the dot. Then instruct them to fold and glue the spur ends together along the edge, leaving the long sides open. To wear, students slip each spur onto their boot (or shoe), as shown.

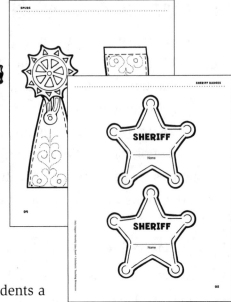

Sheriff Badge

Photocopy the badges (page 95) onto yellow paper. Give students a badge to cut out and label with their name. Then have them use a piece of rolled tape to attach the badge to their shirt.

 ## READING ROUND-UP

Have students complete the report form on page 96 to write about the Wild-West books they have read. In their summary, encourage students to include information about main characters, setting(s), key events, and the climax and resolution of the story. (They can use the back of the page if they need more space to write.) Invite students to share their reports with the class.

 ## WANTED POSTERS

Students can use a Wild-West style "Wanted" poster as a fun way to share information about themselves. Distribute photocopies of the poster on page 97. To start, have students write their name and alias (nickname) on the first two lines and draw a self-portrait in the box. (Or, they might glue a school photo in the box.) Then have students fill out the personal information or dictate their responses for you to write. Once finished, invite students to share their "Wanted" bulletins with the class. If desired, display the posters on a bulletin board or scattered on walls, windows, and doors around the classroom.

★ COWBOY SKILLS WHEEL

Use the cowboy wheel patterns on pages 98–99 to reinforce math skills and more. To prepare, write a problem in each of the large boxes (outlined in gray) on the wheel. Write the answer in the small box directly opposite each problem on the right. Cut out the cowboy, horsetail, and wheel. Then carefully cut out the "windows" on the cowboy pattern. Use one brass fastener to attach the wheel to the cowboy and another to attach the tail, as shown. To use, students turn the wheel so that a problem appears in the left window. They solve the problem and then slide the tail away from the right window to check their answer.

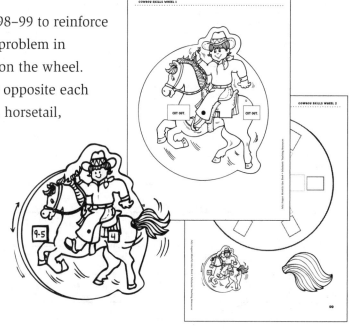

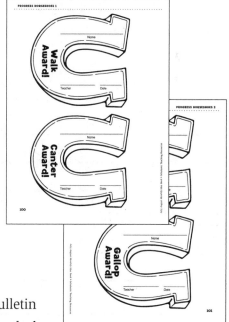

★ PROGRESS HORSESHOES

Explain to students that the four gaits of a horse are walk, canter, trot, and gallop. Then tell them that they will earn horseshoes labeled with these terms to help track their progress toward pre-established goals, such as completing work or reading a specific number of books. First, photocopy and cut out a supply of the horseshoes on pages 100 and 101. Put all of the "Walk" horseshoes in one resealable plastic bag, the "Canter" horseshoes in another bag, and so on. Then set the bags in a basket or box placed in an easy-to-reach location.

To use, whenever a student reaches an agreed-upon step toward a specific goal, fill out a horseshoe and present it to the student, following this order: Walk, Canter, Trot, and Gallop. Have students display their horseshoes on a special bulletin board or keep them in a personal space, such as their cubby or desk. Once a student has met the pre-established criteria for achieving a goal and has collected all four horseshoes, present him or her with a reward, such as a small treat or a special privilege.

July/August Monthly Idea Book © Scholastic Teaching Resources

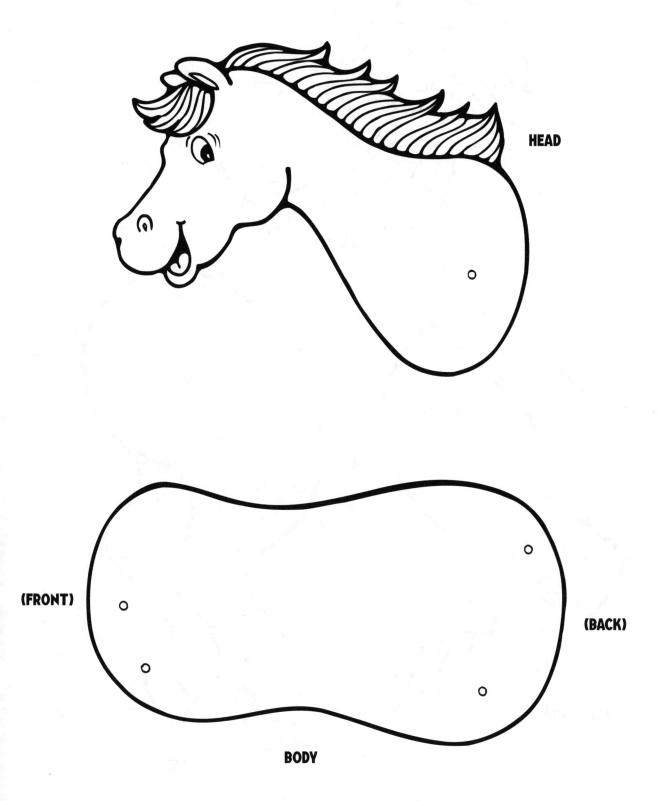

HEAD

(FRONT)

(BACK)

BODY

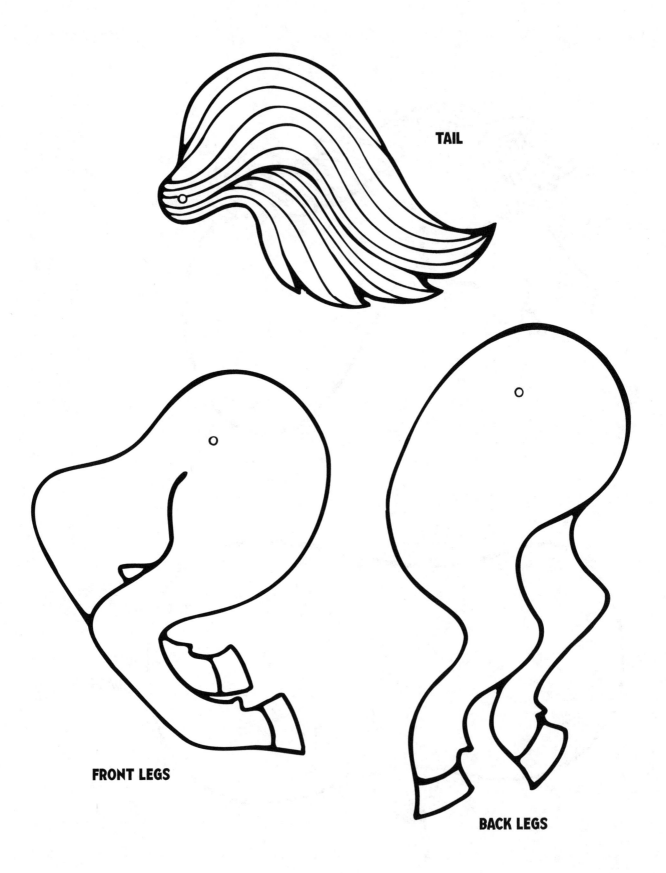

TAIL

FRONT LEGS

BACK LEGS

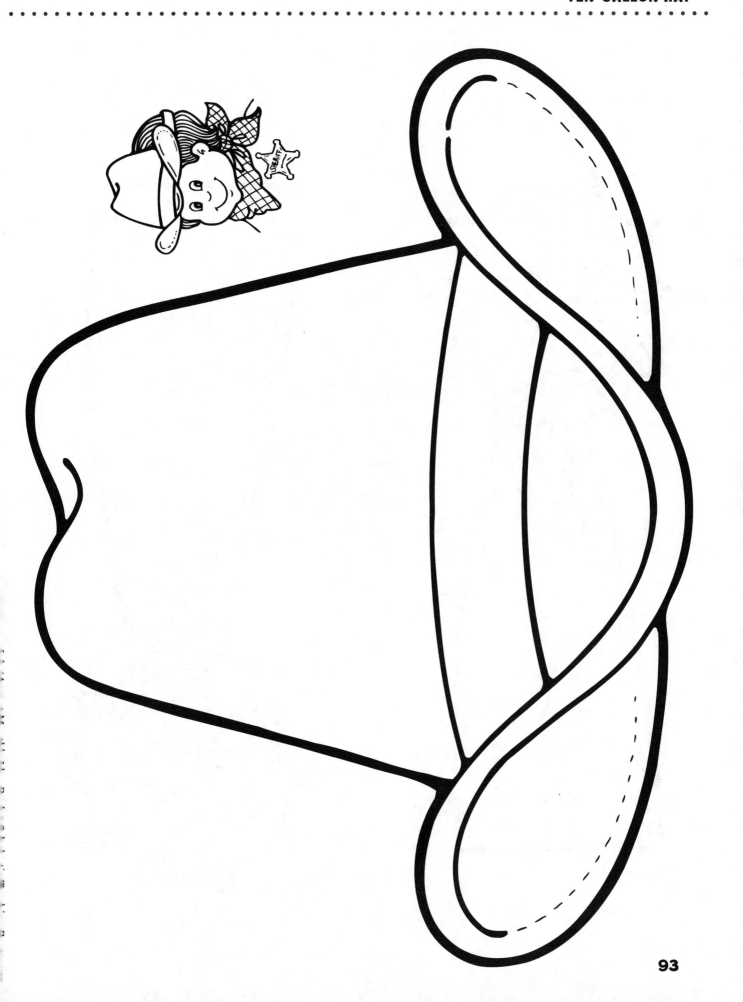

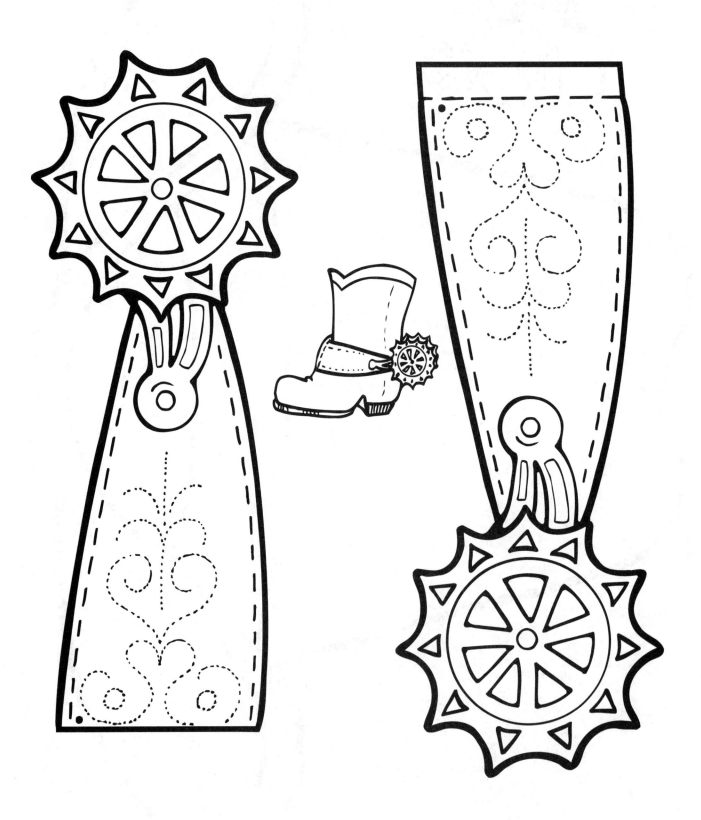

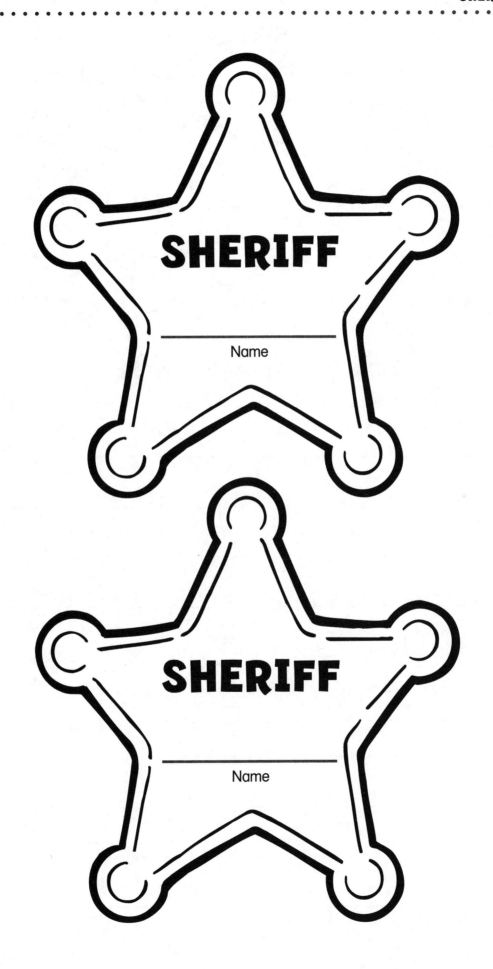

SHERIFF

Name

SHERIFF

Name

Reading Round-Up

Book Title: _____

Author: _____

Main Character: _____

_____

Summary: _____

_____

_____

_____

_____

I liked the book: ☐ yes ☐ no

Why? _____

_____

_____

_____

_____

July/August Monthly Idea Book © Scholastic Teaching Resources

WANTED

$1,000,000 REWARD!

My Picture

Name: _____

Alias: _____

Date Last Seen: _____

Last Known Address: _____

Last Seen Wearing: _____

_____

Age: _____ Birth Date: _____ Eye Color: _____ Hair Color: _____

Known to Hang Out With: _____

_____

Hobbies: _____

Favorite Subjects: _____

Accused of: _____

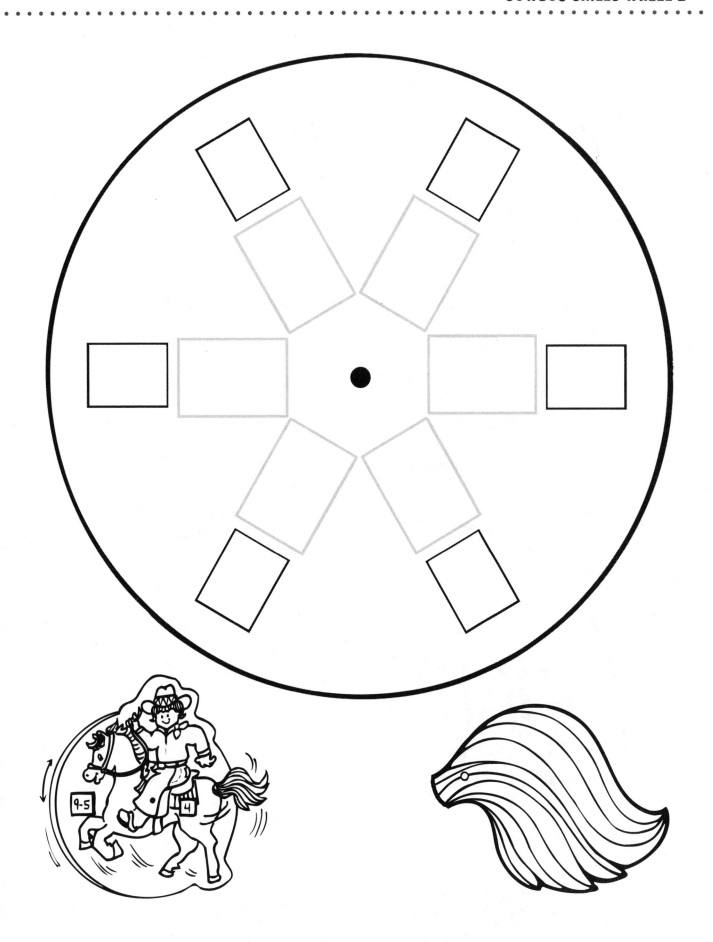

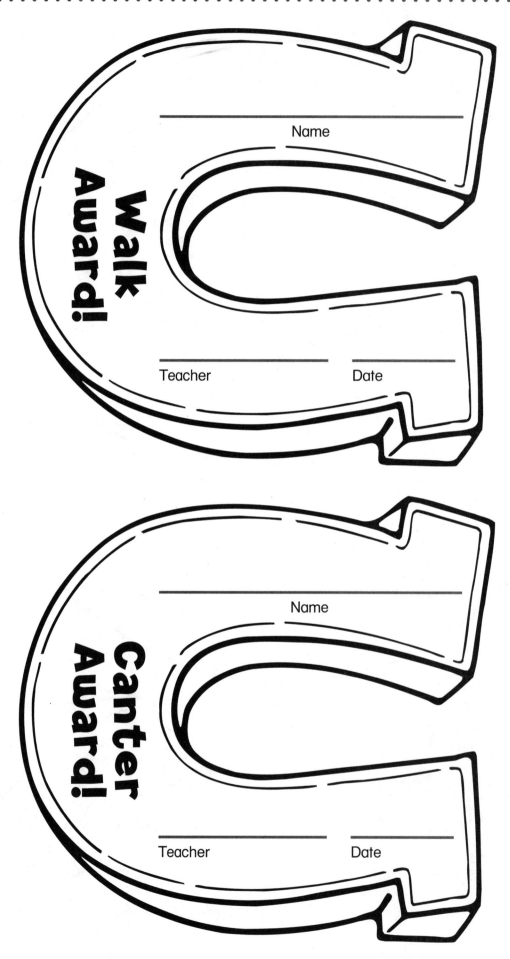

Walk Award!

Name

Teacher

Date

Canter Award!

Name

Teacher

Date

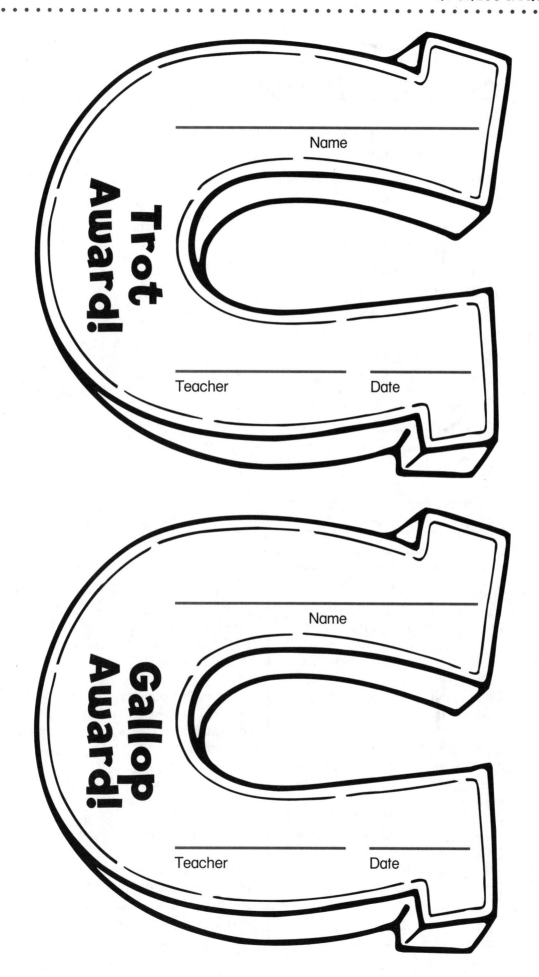

Name

Trot Award!

Teacher   Date

Name

Gallop Award!

Teacher   Date

OUR SOLAR SYSTEM

The Sun, planets and their satellites (or moons), and various other space objects make up our solar system. The word *solar* comes from the Latin word *sol*, meaning sun. Eight planets in our solar system revolve around the Sun. Earth, the third planet from the Sun, has only one moon, but other planets, such as Jupiter and Saturn, may have numerous moons. In addition to the eight planets and their moons, other space objects that exist in our solar system include asteroids, meteors, and comets.

The following chart contains information about each of the planets in our solar system. Terrestrial planets are composed of rock and minerals, while the giant gas planets are composed of gaseous material and do not have solid surfaces.

Planet Facts	
Terrestrial Planets	**Gas Giants**
Mercury: This planet is the smallest, but closest to the Sun. Mercury travels around the Sun faster than any of the other planets. **Venus:** This planet is second from the Sun and is the third brightest object in the sky— only the Sun and moon are brighter. A day on Venus is longer than its year. **Earth:** The only planet known to have life on it, Earth is covered mostly with water. This planet is the third planet from the Sun and has one moon. **Mars:** The fourth planet from the Sun, Mars is also called the Red Planet. This planet is home to the largest volcano in the Solar System. Mars has two moons.	**Jupiter:** The fifth planet from the Sun, Jupiter is the largest of the eight planets. The Great Red Spot on Jupiter is a giant hurricane-like storm. This planet has more than 65 moons. **Saturn:** This planet is the sixth from the Sun and the second largest. Saturn can be identified by its rings and has more than 60 moons. **Uranus:** The coldest of all the planets in our solar system, Uranus spins around the Sun on its side. This planet has 27 moons and is the seventh planet from the Sun. **Neptune:** Storm winds on this planet can blow at speeds up to 1,250 miles per hour. Neptune is the farthest planet from the Sun and has 13 known moons.

Suggested Activities

★ SPACE WORD FIND

Distribute copies of the word find on page 107. Explain to students that the word bank on the page contains words associated with space and space travel. Review the words, then ask students to find and circle each one in the puzzle. After students complete the puzzle, have them unscramble the planet names at the bottom of the page.

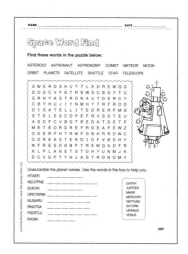

★ SOLAR SYSTEM MOBILE

Students can use these mobiles to share their knowledge of the names and sequence of the planets in our solar system. First, photocopy a class set of the sun and planet patterns on pages 108–110. Distribute a set of the patterns, one 6-inch length of yarn, and eight 2-inch lengths of yarn to each student. Ask students to color and cut out their patterns. Then have them sequence their planet cutouts, from nearest to farthest distance from the Sun, and number the back of each one accordingly. To assemble their mobile, instruct students to use the 2-inch lengths of yarn and tape to connect the planets in order, as shown. (They should tape the ends of the yarn to the back of their cutouts.). Finally, have them attach the 6-inch length of yarn to the top of the Sun to create a hanger. After students share their mobiles with the class, suspend them from the ceiling for all to enjoy. Or, if you prefer, add another 6-inch length of yarn to Neptune and display the mobiles horizontally in a garland-like fashion.

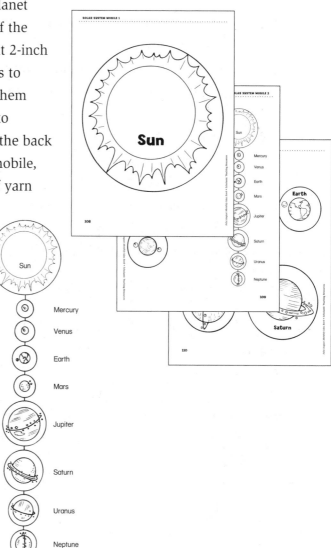

★ MY PLANET REPORT

List the eight planets on chart paper, then review the planet names and information about each one with students. (See the "Planet Facts" chart on page 102.) Afterward, have students choose a planet from the list and do research to learn more about it. They can use nonfiction books, the Internet, documentary videos, and other sources to gather information. Distribute photocopies of page 111 for students to use to record their findings. When finished, invite students to share what they learned about their planet with the class.

★ SPACE STATIONERY AND BOOK COVER

Liven up writing assignments with stationery ideal for writing about space, the solar system, space travel, astronauts, or any other related topic. Students might write poems, songs, acrostics, or imaginary stories. Distribute copies of the stationery on page 112 for students to use for their final drafts. Then invite volunteers to share their written work with small groups or the whole class.

For a finishing touch on students' space writing assignments or research projects, have them use page 113 to create a book cover. Students simply color and cut out the pattern, then glue it to a folded sheet of 11- by 17-inch construction paper where indicated. Finally, they add a title and author line to complete their cover.

★ OUT-OF-THIS-WORLD WORDS

In your writing center, create a display featuring space-related words that students can use in their writing assignments. To prepare, cover a display board with dark paper and add a border. Cut out large, yellow stars and label each with a different word, choosing words that you want students to learn and use in their writing. Attach the stars to the display and add the title "Out-of-This-World Words." If desired, add related art, such as a spaceship or an astronaut.

★ HINGED ASTRONAUT

Invite students to make these astronauts
to use in their presentation, to
display with their research or written
work, or as props for role-playing
and dramatizations. First, distribute
photocopies of pages 114–116 to
students. Ask them to color and cut
out their patterns. Then help students
assemble their astronauts, as shown,
using five brass fasteners to attach the
different parts to the body. To create a

display, students can write space-related facts on large star cutouts
and post them on a bulletin board covered with black paper. Then they
can add their astronauts to the display. Alternately, students might attach
a wide craft stick to the back of their astronaut to use as a handle. They
can then move their astronaut in a variety of ways to make it dance or to
spin and wiggle its arms and legs in amusing ways.

★ SPACE BINGO

Reinforce space-related vocabulary words with a game of
Bingo! To prepare, make several photocopies of the game
board on page 117 and a single copy of the game cards on
pages 118–119. On each game board, fill in the boxes with the
names of different space words that appear on the game cards.
Use a different combination of words on each game board.

Copy the programmed game boards, making enough for each
student in a group (or the whole class) to have one. Next, copy
and cut out the game cards. Finally, laminate all of the game
boards and cards. To play, supply players with Bingo chips or
dried beans to use as markers, then have a caller choose one
word card at a time to read to players. If players have that word on
their game board, they cover it with a marker. Continue play until one
player (or more) has covered all of the words on his or her game board
and calls out "Bingo!"

★ ASTRONAUT SKILLS WHEEL

Use the astronaut wheel patterns on pages 120–121 to reinforce math skills and more. To prepare, write a problem in each of the large boxes (outlined in gray) on the wheel. Write the answer in the small box directly opposite each problem on the right. Cut out the astronaut, flag, and wheel. Then carefully cut out the "windows" on the astronaut. Use one brass fastener to attach the wheel to the astronaut and another to attach the flag, as shown. To use, students turn the wheel so that a problem appears in the left window. They solve the problem and then slide the flag away from the right window to check their answer.

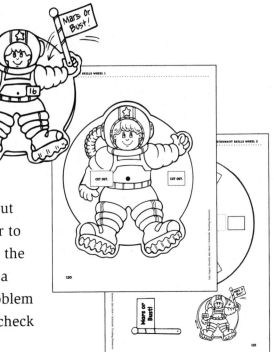

★ SPACESHIP TASK CARDS

Reinforce the skills your students are learning with flash cards that fit the theme of this unit. Simply photocopy the cards on page 122 and cut them out. You can program the cutouts for use as flash cards to teach:

- letters

- numbers

- math facts

- content-area vocabulary words

- sight words

- word families

The cards are ideal for learning-center activities, but you might also use them to label job charts, group students, and more. To store, just put them in a resealable plastic bag.

Space Word Find

Find these words in the puzzle below:

ASTEROID   ASTRONAUT   ASTRONOMY   COMET   METEOR   MOON
ORBIT   PLANETS   SATELLITE   SHUTTLE   STAR   TELESCOPE

```
S  W  E  R  D  S  H  U  T  T  L  E  D  R  E  W  Q  G
D  O  D  C  V  F  G  T  R  E  W  S  C  B  G  Y  T  U
S  R  H  Y  A  S  T  R  O  N  A  U  T  D  E  R  C  Y
C  B  Y  H  U  J  I  Y  N  M  H  Y  T  R  F  R  O  D
D  I  S  A  T  E  L  L  I  T  E  D  R  E  R  F  M  G
S  T  E  L  E  S  C  O  P  E  F  R  V  S  G  T  E  U
A  S  D  F  C  V  B  G  T  R  E  D  A  T  D  E  T  F
M  E  T  E  O  R  D  R  E  F  R  G  E  A  F  E  W  Z
O  D  E  R  F  H  T  R  W  F  G  B  H  R  R  D  W  C
O  D  R  E  A  S  T  E  R  O  I  D  F  V  B  G  H  Y
N  F  R  E  S  D  G  B  F  T  R  E  W  Q  A  D  F  R
K  L  P  L  A  N  E  T  S  T  G  H  Y  U  N  M  J  K
D  C  V  G  F  T  Y  H  J  A  S  T  R  O  N  O  M  Y
```

Unscramble the planet names. Use the words in the box to help you.

HTAER   __ __ __ __ __

NEUTPNE   __ __ __ __ __ __ __

SUEVN   __ __ __ __ __

URCYERM   __ __ __ __ __ __ __

NUSARU   __ __ __ __ __ __

RNUTSA   __ __ __ __ __ __

PIERTUJ   __ __ __ __ __ __ __

RASM   __ __ __ __

EARTH
JUPITER
MARS
MERCURY
NEPTUNE
SATURN
URANUS
VENUS

July/August Monthly Idea Book © Scholastic Teaching Resources

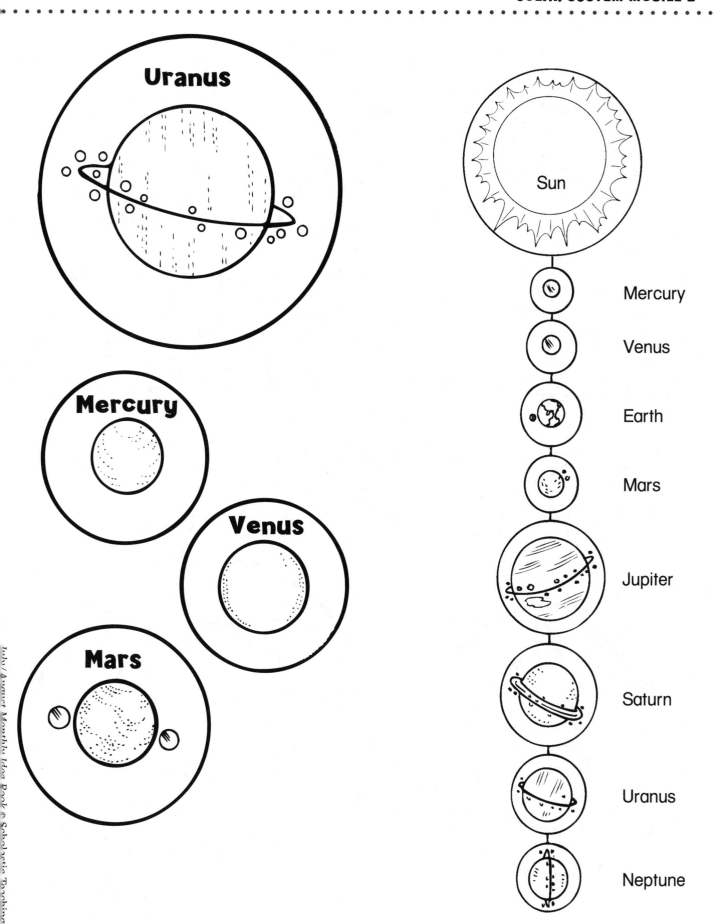

Uranus

Mercury

Venus

Mars

Sun

Mercury

Venus

Earth

Mars

Jupiter

Saturn

Uranus

Neptune

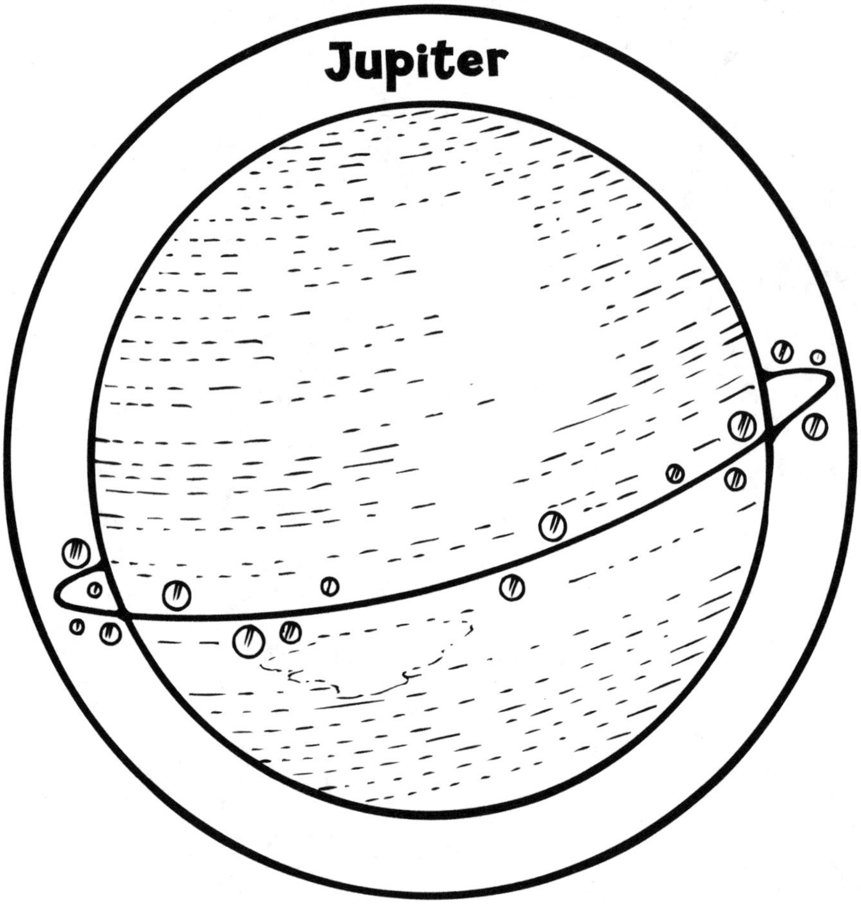

Jupiter

Earth

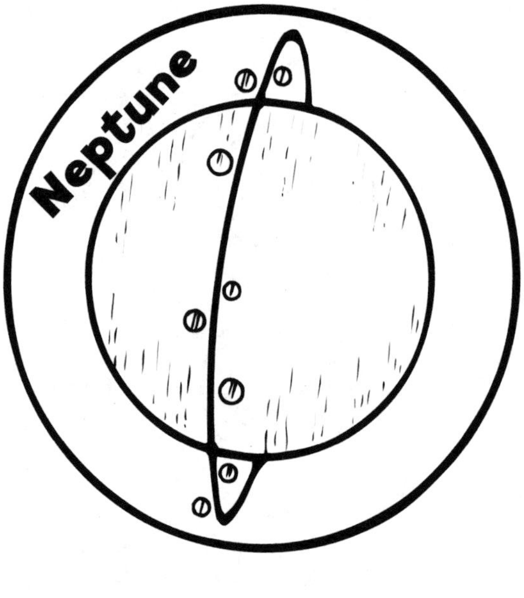

Neptune

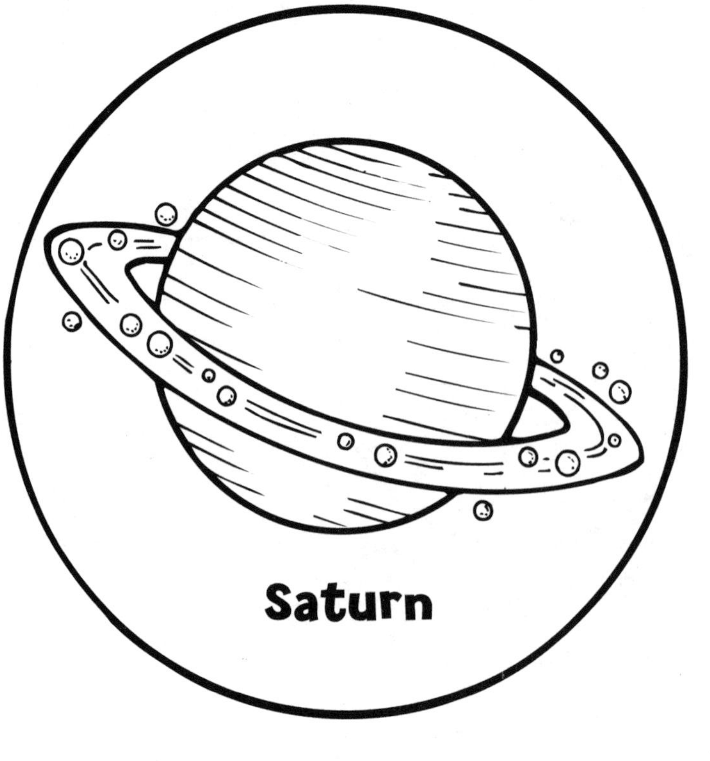

Saturn

My Planet Report

My planet: _____

Distance from the Sun: _____

Size/diameter of my planet: _____

Number of moons: _____

Surface temperature: _____

This is a picture of my planet.

Some interesting facts about my planet are _____

_____

_____

_____

_____

_____

Write a story about what it might be like to visit your planet.

Use the back of this page.

PLACE THIS SIDE ALONG FOLD.

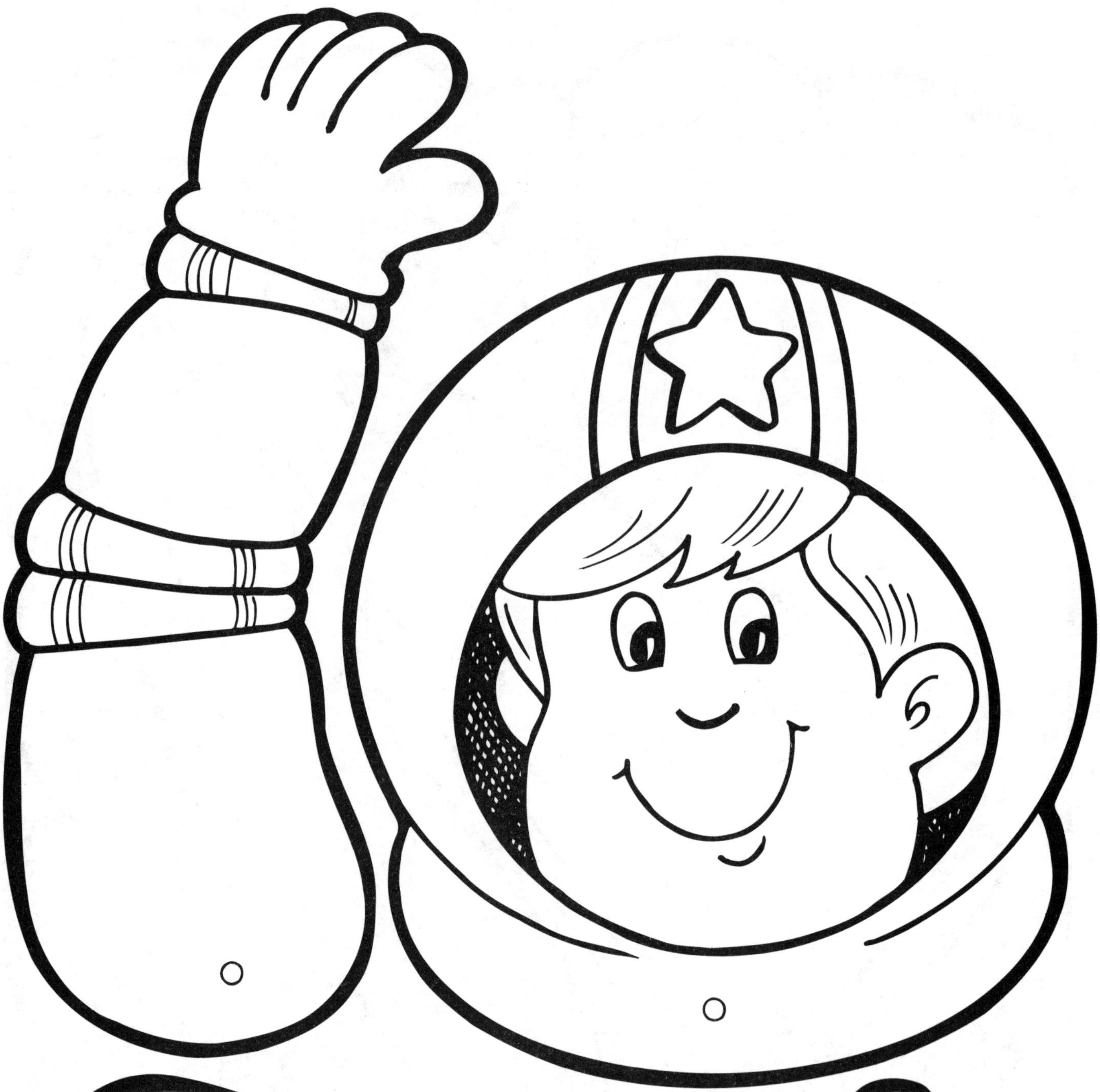

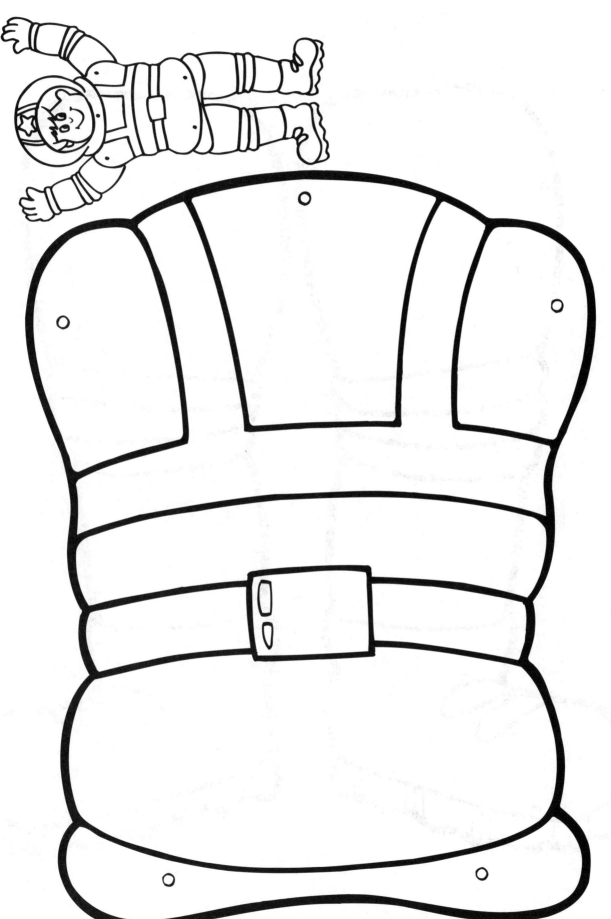

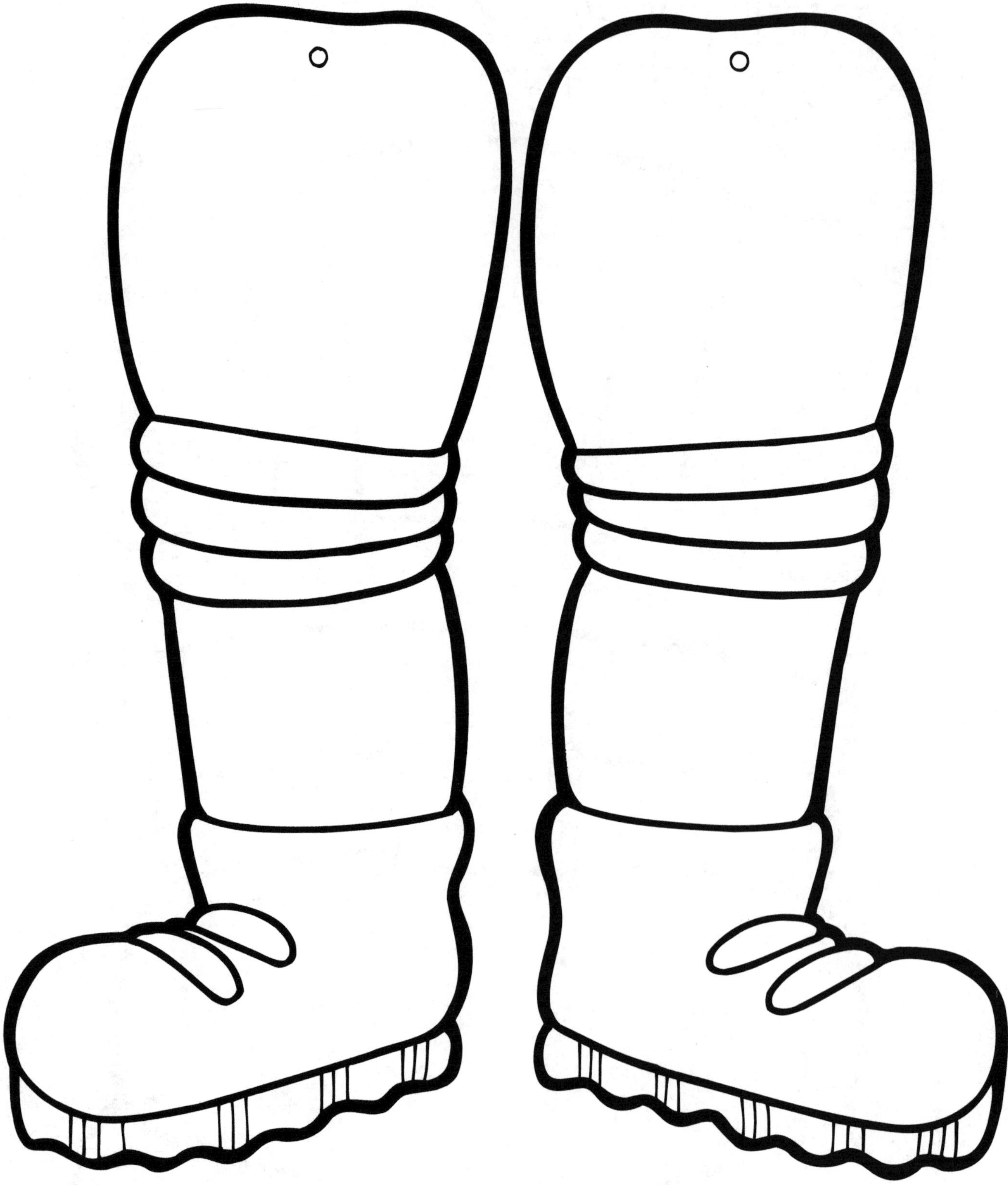

SPACE
BINGO

FREE

Apollo	asteroid	astronaut	astronomy
atmosphere	*Challenger*	comet	constellation
countdown	crew	*Discovery*	Earth
Explorer	flight	galaxy	gravity
Jupiter	launch	lunar	Mars

Mercury	meteor	moon	NASA
Neptune	observatory	orbit	planet
rocket	rotate	satellite	Saturn
solar	space shuttle	space station	star
Sun	telescope	Uranus	Venus

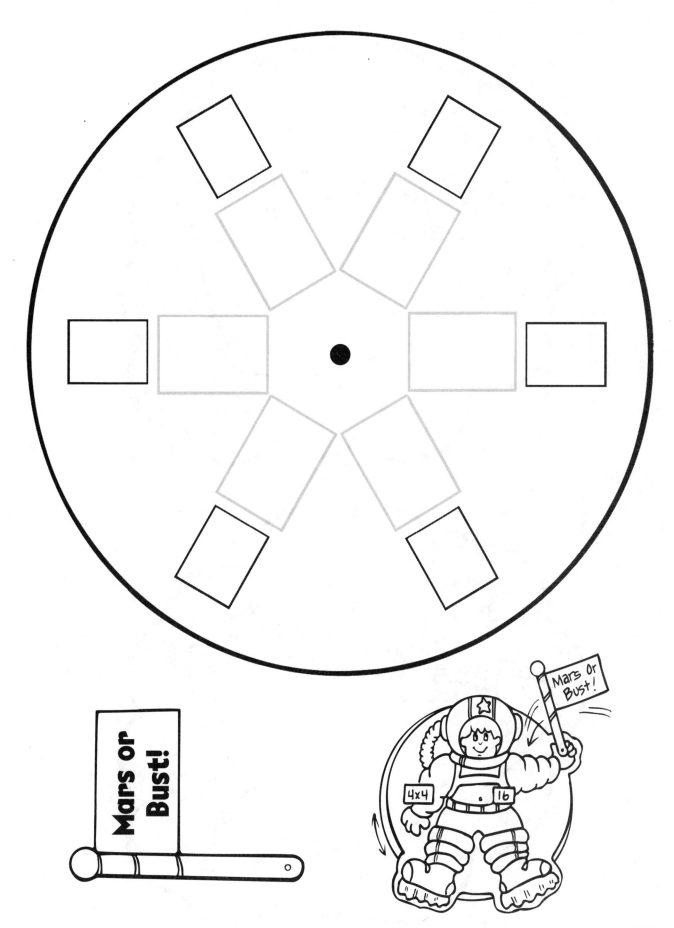

Mars or Bust!

Mars or Bust!

4x4   16

GOOD AND NUTRITIOUS!

During the summer, preparing for a new school year, or any time is the right time to focus on nutrition. Developing healthy eating habits and learning to choose nutritious foods are skills that will serve students in a positive way throughout their lives. In addition to the activities in this unit, you can visit www.choosemyplate.gov to gather more information about the five food groups and find tips for building healthier diets. You can also download the new MyPlate place-setting image—provided by the United States Department of Agriculture—to help students identify which food groups their meal and snack foods fit into.

Suggested Activities

★ THE FIVE FOOD GROUPS

Tell students that the five main food groups are fruits, grains, proteins, vegetables, and dairy. Write each group name on chart paper and have students brainstorm foods that belong to each one. Afterward, review the food cards on pages 127–129, then distribute photocopies of the cards along with five nine-inch paper plates to each student. Help students label each of their plates with a different food group. Then have them color and cut out their cards. Afterward, instruct students to sort the food cards onto their plates according to the groups they belong to. When finished, invite students to share and compare their food groupings to check that they sorted them correctly. Finally, have students glue the cards to the plates. Encourage them to take the plates home to share with their family.

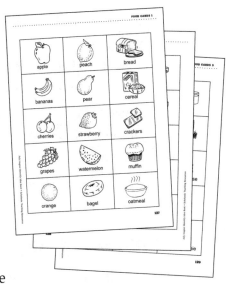

FOOD GROUP GAMES

Color, cut out, and laminate a set of the food cards used in "The Five Food Groups" on page 123. Use the cards for the following games to help reinforce students' knowledge about the different food groups:

■ **Memory:** Choose four cards from each food group (two pairs per group). Shuffle and place the cards facedown to form a 4- by 5-card grid. Then invite two or three students to play Memory, trying to find two foods that belong to the same food group. Players take turns until they find all of the matches. The player with the most matches wins the game.

■ **Go Fish:** Two to five students can play this modified card game. To set up, shuffle the food cards and distribute five cards to each player. Stack the remaining cards facedown. To play, have players follow the general rules of Go Fish, asking other players for cards from particular food groups, such as "Do you have a protein?" The first player to collect five cards from one food group, such as five grains, wins the game.

■ **Food Recall**: Place several food cards faceup on a tray. (The foods might belong to the same food group or different groups.) Show the tray of cards to students for a brief period of time, telling them to study and try to memorize the foods on display. Then remove the tray from the students' view and challenge them to name from memory as many of the foods as possible. Afterward, display the tray again so students can check their response. As an alternative, display the cards, then ask students to close their eyes as you remove a few cards from the tray. Finally, have students try to name the missing foods.

IMPORTANT NUTRIENTS

Give students photocopies of page 130, then explain the importance of including foods in their diet that contain nutrients, such as the ones shown on their sheet. Review the nutrients and why they are important. Then have students do research to try to find three foods that contain each nutrient. Have them write their findings on the lines next to each nutrient.

MY DAILY DIET

To help students keep track of the foods they eat on a daily basis, have them keep a record of their meals and snacks for a week. Distribute a week's supply of page 131 to each student. Instruct them to fill in the foods they eat each day, then determine how many foods from each food group they consumed that day. Have them record their findings at the bottom of the page. At the end of the week, invite students to share about their daily diets and discuss ways they might improve their food choices or nutrition habits.

NUTRITIOUS WRITING

Invite students to use the stationery on page 132 when writing about healthy food and nutrition. They might write poems, short stories, or songs about the five food groups, the nutritious value of particular foods, and so on. Or they might write a recipe for their favorite nutritious food or directions on how to make a sandwich that contains healthy ingredients.

To display their written work, ask students to color and cut out photocopies of the chef page-framer patterns on page 133, then glue the patterns to the edges of a sheet of construction paper. They can then glue their written work to the page framer. Or, if desired, have students use page 134 to create a book cover for their writing assignments. To make, students color and cut out the pattern, glue it to a folded sheet of 11- by 17-inch construction paper where indicated, then add a title and name line.

MENU CHALLENGE

This quick-and-easy activity will encourage students to make nutritious considerations in choosing foods when eating out. First, collect and bring in a variety of menus from chain restaurants, delis, and fast-food eateries. Ask student pairs or small groups to select a menu and then choose foods from that menu to assemble healthy meals, including foods from as many of the food groups as possible. When finished, discuss the meal ensembles and talk about the food groups represented in each one. As a follow-up activity, have students create their own menus that include healthy foods from each of the five food groups.

★ CHEF'S HAT

Students can make their own chef's hat to use when making their presentations or for role-playing activities. To begin, give students a 10- by 24-inch sheet of white bulletin board paper. Help them form a tube from their paper, fitting the long edge around their head and taping the ends in place, as shown. Then have students cut one-inch slits around the top end of the tube so that it resembles a chef's hat.

★ HAMBURGER MOBILE

Hamburgers have been longtime favorites of kids and adults alike. Invite students to make this hamburger mobile to discover which food groups are represented on this sandwich. Give each student a photocopy of the hamburger patterns (page 135), one 6-inch length of yarn, and six 2-inch lengths of yarn. Help students name each ingredient on their page, then have them color and cut out the patterns. Next, instruct them to label the back of each pattern with the food group that the item pictured on the front belongs to. To assemble, have students use the 2-inch lengths of yarn to attach the hamburger ingredients to each other, "stacking" them in any order between the top and bottom buns. Finally, have them add the 6-inch length of yarn to the top of the bun top to make a hanger. (If desired, students might make their own ingredients to add to their mobile.)

 apple	 peach	 bread
 bananas	 pear	 cereal
 cherries	 strawberry	 crackers
 grapes	 watermelon	 muffin
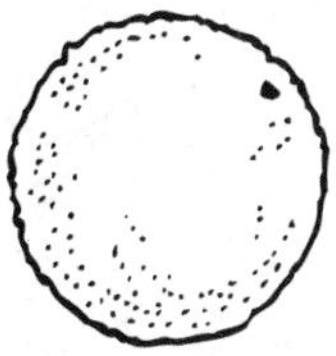 orange	 bagel	 oatmeal

pasta	chicken	tuna
pretzel	eggs	turkey
rice	fish	asparagus
almonds	nuts	beans
beef	pork	broccoli

July/August Monthly Idea Book © Scholastic Teaching Resources

carrot

tomato

milk

corn

American cheese

soy milk

peas

chocolate milk

Swiss cheese

spinach

cottage cheese

yogurt

squash

ice cream

yogurt smoothie

Important Nutrients

List some foods that contain each of the following nutrients:

 **Vitamin A** increases resistance to infection and helps improve eyesight.

_____

_____

_____

 **Vitamin B** aids in good digestion and steady nerves.

_____

_____

_____

 **Vitamin C** prevents scurvy and helps our muscles and gums.

_____

_____

_____

 **Vitamin D** helps keep our teeth and bones healthy and strong.

_____

_____

_____

 **Carbohydrates** give us strength and energy.

_____

_____

_____

 **Proteins** help build and repair our bodies.

_____

_____

_____

July/August Monthly Idea Book • Scholastic Teaching Resources

My Daily Diet

Breakfast:

_____   _____

_____   _____

_____   _____

Lunch:

_____   _____

_____   _____

_____   _____

Dinner:

_____   _____

_____   _____

_____   _____

Snacks:

_____   _____

_____   _____

_____   _____

Record how many servings you ate from each food group:

	Grains		Dairy		Vegetables

	Proteins		Fruits

PLACE THIS SIDE ALONG FOLD.

AWARDS, INCENTIVES, AND MORE

Getting Started

Make several photocopies of the reproducibles on pages 138 through 142. Giving out the bookmarks, pencil toppers, notes, and certificates will show students your enthusiasm for their efforts and achievements. Plus, bookmarks and pencil toppers are a fun treat for students celebrating birthdays.

■ Provide materials for decorating, including markers, color pencils, and stickers.

■ Encourage students to bring home their creations to share and celebrate with family members.

★ BOOKMARKS

1. Photocopy onto tagboard and cut apart.

2. For more fanfare, punch a hole on one end and tie on a length of colorful ribbon or yarn.

★ PENCIL TOPPERS

1. Photocopy onto tagboard and cut out.

2. Use an art knife to cut through the Xs.

3. Slide a pencil through the Xs as shown.

SEND-HOME NOTES

1. Photocopy and cut apart.

2. Record the child's name and the date.

3. Add your signature.

4. Add more details about the student's day on the back of the note.

CERTIFICATES

1. Photocopy.

2. Record the child's name and other information, as directed.

3. Add details about the child's achievement (if applicable), then add your signature and the date.

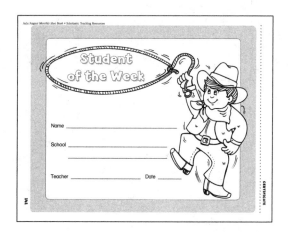

Stay cool! Visit the library!

Dreams come true when you READ!

DISCOVER LIBERTY IN THE LIBRARY

Student's Name

You
are my
sunshine!

Did a great job today!

Teacher   Date

Student's Name

was SUPER today!

Way to go!

Teacher   Date

Student's Name

Did a "yummy" job!

Teacher   Date

Student's Name

was a real winner today!

Teacher   Date

Student
of the Week

Name _____

School _____

Teacher _____

Date _____

Certificate of Achievement

presented to

_____

Name

in recognition of

_____

Teacher

_____

Date

July/August Monthly Idea Book © Scholastic Teaching Resources

Patriotic Fun Word Find, page 61

```
X C F T R E V F R E E D O M D F T Y
D F L D T Y G H J U S E T E O U L K
F Y A R G T Y J U S T I C E D E W R
W O G F G T Y H J U I K L O P H J S
P A T R I O T I S M S W Q E R T Y T
S D F R T G G D E D S E W D S W T A
F B V C X L T Y U I L I B E R T Y R
F B V C X O F A M E R I C A D R E S
D C V F G R G T H D E S E S A E T T
C V B F G Y D R E F G T H Y U J K R
U N C L E S A M D R F G T Y H J U I
H S D R R E G V B N M J H K I U J P
O G D E C L A R A T I O N D F R T E
N F V G B H N J M K L O I K J M N S
O V B G F B A Z J H R I G H T S G L
R C V B H G N M J K L O I K M J N H
Q R I N D E P E N D E N C E P L M T
Z E Q U A L I T Y M X P O L T R F E
```

The Great American Symbol, page 73

Connect the dots, starting at 1.
What American symbol did you draw?
Spell the name of the symbol on the lines.

THE

S T A T U E

OF

L I B E R T Y

Space Word Find, page 107

```
S W E R D S H U T T L E D R E W Q G
D O D C V F G T R E W S C B G Y T U
S R H Y A S T R O N A U T D E R C Y
C B Y H U J I Y N M H Y T R F R O D
D I S A T E L L I T E D R E R F M G
S T E L E S C O P E F R V S G T E U
A S D F C V B G T R E D A T D E T T
M E T E O R D R E F R G E A F E W Z
O D E R F H T R W F G B H R D W C
O D R E A S T E R O I D F V B G H Y
N F R E S D G B F T R E W Q A D F R
K L P L A N E T S T G H Y U N M J K
D C V G F T Y H J A S T R O N O M Y
```

Unscramble the planet names.

HTAER	E A R T H		
NEUTPNE	N E P T U N E		
SUEVN	V E N U S		
URCYERM	M E R C U R Y		
NUSARU	U R A N U S		
RNUTSA	S A T U R N		
PIERTUJ	J U P I T E R		
RASM	M A R S		